D1303504

ANOTHER SPLASH

ANOTHER SPLASH OF THE GIN & TONIC GARDENER

OF THE

Further Confessions of a Reformed Compulsive Gardener

JANICE WELLS

KEY PORTER BOOKS

Library and Archives Canada Cataloguing in Publication

Wells, Janice, 1948-
    Another splash of the gin & tonic gardener / by Janice Wells.

ISBN 978-1-55263-991-7

    1. Wells, Janice, 1948- —Anecdotes. 2. Gardening—Humor. 3. Low maintenance gardening—Newfoundland and Labrador. I. Title.

SB473.W44 2008   635.9   C2007-906425-6

THE CANADA COUNCIL | LE CONSEIL DES ARTS
FOR THE ARTS | DU CANADA
SINCE 1957 | DEPUIS 1957

ONTARIO ARTS COUNCIL
CONSEIL DES ARTS DE L'ONT

The publisher gratefully acknowledges the support of the Canada Council for the Arts and the Ontario Arts Council for its publishing program. We acknowledge the support of the Government of Ontario through the Ontario Media Development Corporation's Ontario Book Initiative.

We acknowledge the financial support of the Government of Canada through the Book Publishing Industry Development Program (BPIDP) for our publishing activities.

Key Porter Books Limited
Six Adelaide Street East, Tenth Floor
Toronto, Ontario
Canada M5C 1H6
www.keyporter.com

Design: Martin Gould
Electronic Formatting: Alison Carr

Illustrations: Mel D'Souza
Printed and bound in Canada

08 09 10 11 12 6 5 4 3 2 1

Contents

To Mom and Dad with Love

Itching to Get Started

MAY 2000

Surfing the garden Web will never replace browsing in garden magazines for me, but I must confess there is a whole wonderful garden world inside the laptop I not so affectionately call Damian (spawn of the devil). On this early May day, listening to freezing sleet on my window and putting another log on the fire, I wanted a garden fix so badly I just had to resort to Damian.

The website www.icangarden.com led me to more sites than I could possibly look at in one day, and I picked up all kinds of design tips. I found a great idea for a rustic frame for sunflowers and another for making a "gnome" garden door out of an old house door. There was how to improve the look of concrete by staining it, how to make new wood look aged, garden sculpture from old car springs, and a birdbath from fifteen wine bottles and a garbage can lid! That was about the time I gave up, but I'm sure I'll be back.

The sunflower frame is an excellent idea for the giants I might try for the birds this year. I say might because as much as I'd love to have a few sunflowers, there's a great demand for the sunny spots in my garden. The frame is tempting me, though, because I love garden architecture almost as much as I love sun-loving plants. It would not only provide support, but also look good, especially made from fat alder branches or thin unpeeled spruce.

The gnome door, flanked by sections of fencing, made me look with a new eye at some doors I have stored in the basement. The worn lower section of an exterior door was simply cut off. Whimsical ants were painted crawling over the door and a piece of board nailed to the top made a ledge for a planter and bird feeder. You could easily imagine the stunted door surrounded by tumbling plants and climbing vines, leading to a gnome's cottage. I'm thinking the idea could translate easily to a faux root cellar on my upper bank.

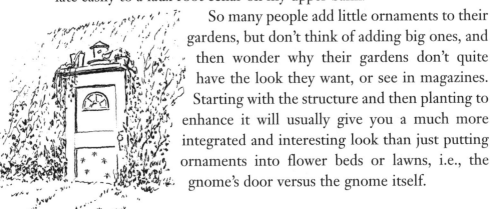

So many people add little ornaments to their gardens, but don't think of adding big ones, and then wonder why their gardens don't quite have the look they want, or see in magazines. Starting with the structure and then planting to enhance it will usually give you a much more integrated and interesting look than just putting ornaments into flower beds or lawns, i.e., the gnome's door versus the gnome itself.

Me, I subscribe to the philosophy that beauty is in the eye of the beholder and you should put whatever you like in your garden, but if you've seen a look that you like and can't quite put your finger on how to get it in your own garden, garden architecture and scale may be the secret.

Even if you have a small garden, bigger is better when it comes to a focal point. I don't mean gigantic (unless, of course, you really like gigantic), but one nice size structure will usually please the eye better than a random smattering of smaller ones. A really interesting idea, especially for a tiny garden, is to use an old mirror as a focal point and fool the eye into expanding the size of the space. I've got a big old oval one just waiting for me to glue the frame back together before it's ready to reflect some chosen view and some unsuspecting visitor.

May, unfortunately, is often still dreaming time for Newfoundland gardeners. It's the time to put another log in the wood stove and go through the latest garden catalogues, which you can also do online if, like me, by now you've practically memorized the paper ones you have.

All I did was enter "gardening catalogues" in the search spot, check "Canadian sites only," and I came up with 971 sites! Needless to say, I haven't looked at them all. I think if I had a full-size computer instead of Damian, I might even get hooked, at least through January and February and March. Okay, okay, April is not so great around here either. May can be quite good, but not today.

Northern gardeners are a hardy bunch.

On the Wagon Again

MY MOTHER WOULD BE PROUD. Here I am, at the beginning of planting season, holding impulsiveness in check, and being sensible for a change. That means I'm not out at the nurseries succumbing to the lure of bright green foliage unfurling in perennial pots or buds fattening and popping on twiggy shrubs. By this time last year I had spent many hours and many dollars on things my garden wasn't really ready for. Of course, the terrible weather this year probably has as much to do with my being sensible as my actually *being* sensible, but I like to take credit wherever I can.

You are once again reading the words of a reformed gardener. Or perhaps that should be "you are reading the words of a once again reformed gardener"? This time I really really really have to be practical. With my star boarder, my father, gone now, the only way I can afford to try to be a writer when I grow up and keep this house, which I've only had a year, is to renovate the old apartment in the lower level (I hate to say basement because, being mainly above ground, it doesn't feel like a basement) and move into it myself. I haven't found the money to do it yet, but I will, just you wait and see.

It will be what the English sometimes call a "garden flat," opening on the level right into the back garden and once I'm ensconced in there, with tenants in the main house paying my mortgage, I'll be able to stop worrying about losing the house and moving again.

I like this house. It's a 1920s one-and-a-half storey, set on a steep hill in the west end of downtown St. John's. A central front dormer sits over a full-width verandah. Concrete steps and a path divide the front into two small grassy squares 14 feet deep and 12 and 15 feet wide. The uphill section is sloped, the downhill section has been made level by the use of a concrete retaining wall, which drops about 6 feet to a driveway that slopes all the way back to the rear fence.

The backyard is about 25 feet deep by 50 feet wide. An attempt was made at terracing by some previous stalwart and it is more or less divided into four sections; the largest, about 30 feet long, is the middle section, which is separated from the flat 10-foot section at the end of the driveway by a leaning and crumbling concrete wall and is terraced up into another flat area about 8 feet wide at the top of the yard, which is bordered by a steep 10-foot bank between me and the "up" neighbour. The "down" neighbour's backyard is an 8-foot drop from the rear of my driveway.

An 8-foot wire fence follows the slope from the top down to the retaining wall where it joins a new-looking tall green picket fence at the end of the driveway. The back has southern exposure, but is shaded by too many trees, and on the back upper side of the house, there's a nice deck towering above the garden. I bemoaned that there were no steps from the deck down to the garden, but now that someone else will be living in the house and using that deck, I'm rather glad because the garden will be all mine.

The kitchen door of the old apartment that will be my new apartment opens right into the garden and with new windows all at garden level, I think I'll be quite content there. With new multi-paned windows, a comfy window seat, and a little wood stove with glass doors so I can see the fire, it will become my "cottage."

It's making me look at the garden from a whole new angle. Now the view from the apartment kitchen door and windows will be the important one, not the view from the deck and the upstairs, and I'll have to have my own little deck and a path leading from it through the garden, and steps to the upper level.

Those things are the horse; the garden is the cart. We know which one should come first.

There's Gold in That Thar Barrel

THE DIFFERENCE THAT FEELING settled in a place makes is that while you might still want some instant gratification in the garden, you're more concerned about doing things that will bring years of satisfaction. Mom's lesson no. 1: soil, soil, soil. And if, like me, you have a "garden" made up mainly of weedy, scruffy grass and rocky soil, it's easy to get overwhelmed and just lie down 'til the gardening feeling goes away. Mom's lesson no. 2: start small.

That's the hardest one for me. No one has ever accused me of thinking small, or of being patient either, come to think of it. It's long past time that I learned both, especially now that being badly bent, if not downright broke seems to be my status for the foreseeable future. Having said that, however, I don't want to think small or be patient with compost. I want lots of it, and fast. And, my thrill of the year so far, one of my readers has made me a compost tumbler! (I don't even want to think about what that says about my life.)

I won't get it until next week, but I've seen the drawing, and I know it's going to be every bit as good as one I saw advertised in a gardening magazine. The magazine ad didn't give the price, and I could understand why when I saw they were offering $120 off and a convenient three-month instalment plan!

In a Newfoundland magazine gardening column I remarked that resourceful outport Newfoundland men could probably whip up a compost tumbler from a 45-gallon oil drum in no time, and the next thing you know, I get a fax from a chap who read the column and sat right down and designed one. He calls it The Whip-It.

The idea is that instead of adding things every day and turning it with a garden fork, like you would in an ordinary compost pile, you fill it up, turn it every day, and the compost is ready in two weeks! So you'll need to collect stuff up until you have enough for a load, but you won't have to wait months for the compost. Right now I have bags of leaves from last fall, two-year-old manure, buckets of kitchen peelings, eggshells, coffee grounds, the usual suspects. In a couple of weeks, unfortunately, there'll be grass clippings, so soon after my Whip-It arrives, I'll be able to fill it up, and see what happens.

The manure I got for free at a riding stable, and on my way to pick it up, I happened upon a huge source of the same aged product from cattle, which is even better (and sheep's manure is supposed to be better still, according to my mother, although I don't know why). Manure of any kind is a real find when you live in a city because it supplies a lot of heat, which really speeds up the decomposition process.

My hope is to be able to build up my garden soil without buying costly topsoil and amendments by turning out 45 gallons of compost every two weeks or so. I won't produce enough compostable material myself to do that, so I will be looking for alternate sources, such as seaweed and peaty turf, or maybe contributions from others. That's starting to sound like more work in itself, but I suppose it would be worth it for good compost.

Anyway, if the Whip-It works like it is supposed to, maybe I'll persuade the inventor to start producing them, or at least share the plans. I have to confess it sounds too good to be true, and you know what they say about things that sound too good to be true, but you never know.

Between a Rock and a Hard Place

WHAT A LOVELY TIME I had on the long weekend. I had almost forgotten the immense satisfaction I feel after a day of hard physical labour outdoors. All I did was dig a 3-foot-wide bed along the 30-foot section of wire fence in the back. I want to completely hide this ugly 8-foot high fence. Last season, I planted a Virginia creeper and a firethorn there and then gave up. Every thrust of the shovel seemed to hit solid rock. I managed to wrestle two holes from that stubborn ground, and that was enough for my weary spirit, not to mention body.

This time I attacked with a pickaxe. My fence staggers up the top of a grassed bank that also slopes steeply down on the other side of the fence to the cul-de-sac behind me. It took me a whole day to just get the sods off that strip and what I found, to my great delight, is that someone had buried big flat slabs of stone along my side of the fence—I suppose for retaining purposes—before the grass and tree roots filled in. The stones aren't needed there anymore and I now have some beauties to use for steps, a bonus I wasn't expecting.

When you have a garden with almost nothing in it, deciding what to do first can be enough to turn you off, especially if you have trouble with decision making in the first place. The only thing to do is just pick one spot and start. You'd be amazed at how making that little decision will help you focus.

I know what I want (I've been saying it long enough): "an old-fashioned cottage-style garden that beckons me to enjoy it instead of reproaching me for not working in it; a gin-and-tonic-hammock-good-book kind of garden where nothing is forced to be neat if it doesn't want to be and where I never feel guilty about doing nothing productive" but to say that I'm less definite about how it will evolve here is an understatement to say the least.

That narrow strip is my starting point. I kept it to 3 feet wide because that's the distance between the fence and the trunk of the big maple, and starting off there was a big enough task. But already, after looking at it for a few days, I've decided to work around the trunk, which will add another 3 feet to the width. Then when I go out to a garden centre or visit a friend's garden, I know that whatever I come home with will have at least a temporary home. As I develop the garden, things will get moved around, but at least I won't have to pass up something I want for the garden because I don't have a spot with decent soil ready for it.

For starters, this season, I've sort of decided on American bittersweet and wisteria if my local nursery people agree. They fit my criteria for that fence: twining, fast growing, and shade tolerant. If the wisteria takes off, I'll end up moving the firethorn and hard pruning, or maybe even moving the others, but I'll gladly face that if I have to—anything to cover that fence quickly.

Ultimately, I'll clear a narrow border on the lower and upper sides of the yard, and keep moving inwards until the backyard is my dream garden of old-fashioned roses and perennials with herbs and vegetables all mixed in, overflowing brick pathways and stone steps, with a gate or two and anything else that soothes my spirit. (It is indeed serendipitous that those lovely stones were just waiting for me to unearth them.) Doing the perimeters first will address the privacy issue as quickly as possible and everything else will take place within a more intimate enclave.

Every time I look out my window at that strip of dark bare soil, and I do it often, I marvel at how rich it looks. I was right last year when I complained bitterly about it being full of stones, but what's left when the stones are removed actually looks lovely. Unfortunately, I took out so many rocks that what's left is more of a trench than a bed, so now I have to fill it in.

I have hundreds of caplin in meal-size bags left over from Papa's day, taking up valuable space in the freezer compartment of the refrigerator. They look at me with baleful eyes every time I open the door because they know I don't want to eat them. By the end of next week, they'll be head to tail along the bottom of my trench. Then I'll put a layer of that old manure on top of them, empty a few bags of last year's leaves, and (unfortunately) still have plenty of room for compost and topsoil.

If all goes well, every few weeks, I'll have a drum full of compost to add to the mix. The Whip-Pit arrived and I filled it up on the 23rd. I'm keeping track of what I put in so I can find the best recipe and will let you know how I make out.

5.

Nature's Garden

Weeds are funny things. A weed is really just something growing where it isn't wanted, and when you think about it, that is pretty much in the eye of the beholder. I'm looking at the month of June in the Downhomer calendar. For those of you who don't have this wonderful collection of Newfoundland photographs, June features *Pasadena Pasture* by Wanda Ryan. A little girl, looking much like a flower herself, stands in a field of yellow flowers, sniffing a single blossom. To the eye of this beholder that picture is more beautiful than if the little girl was smelling a rose, surrounded by well-manicured flower beds.

Did I forget to say the flowers are dandelions? To use a good Newfoundland expression, what odds? I'm sure somewhere in the world the dandelion would be as admired as the rose is here.

I fight the dandelion battle in flower beds, but to tell the truth, I find them pretty in lawns. I know that's blasphemy to lawn people, but I'm not one, so there you go. The calendar picture got me thinking of a memorable article I read a few years back about a couple who had bought a charming old farmhouse, surrounded by a wild meadow, vines and brambles, an overgrown piece of woods, and a weedy pond.

Unbelievably, I dug around and found it in *Canadian Gardening*, May 1998, by Sara Stein. (It's not unbelievable that I still had the magazine because I can't throw out a gardening magazine; it's just unbelievable that I was able to find a particular article because, of course, I'm not organized enough to have any cataloging system.)

Anyway, after a few years of working on the house, they turned their attention to making a "proper garden." They finally got rid of the thickets and underbrush, cleared out the brambles, and "mowed every bit of open space so it looked like lawn." Then they planted ornamental trees and shrubs and made flower beds. They kept things nice; grass mowed, leaves raked, hedge clipped, flowers deadheaded.

But they felt something was missing, and finally realized it was the birds in the

morning, the frogs in the evening, the fox in the meadow, the chipmunk under the wall, the grouse, the owl, and the butterflies. What they had done, in their efforts to improve the land to conventional standards for their own habitation, was clear away much of the natural food and shelter of the original, natural inhabitants.

There they were, with a mower and an industrial whipper-snipper, a leaf blower and a back-sprayer, a sprinkler system, a shed full of fertilizers, and more work than fun in their garden. In fact when they wanted a break, they'd get in the car and drive out to enjoy nature somewhere.

They were spending a lot of time and money to maintain a piece of land that had gotten along very well without them until it was "civilized." Their hard work had taken their land from "wild and lively to tame and empty." It looked nice but felt wrong, so they reversed their tactics altogether, starting by cutting out part of the lawn and put in a meadow.

There's a happy medium. You don't have to let your property stay or go completely wild to maintain a good ecological balance. There's also not a whole lot of wilderness you can create out of the average 50 by 100 city lot, but even there a few native plants, a corner thicket, or small meadow border will encourage Nature to live in your garden again.

That was proven to me one bitterly cold day in mid-February. I've always bemoaned the lack of birds in my St. John's garden, even though I have lots of plants and feeders. Imagine my excitement when I looked out my bedroom window and saw a big fat robin, a cedar waxwing, and two purple finches, all munching on some mountain ash berries, left over from an outdoor Christmas wreath I'd made, and just laid on a bench. Earlier in the week the snow had blown or melted off them. The feeders didn't attract the birds, but the red berries sure did. Once the berries were all gone, so were the birds.

I'm so glad Wanda Ryan's picture inspired me to dig out that article (and so tickled with myself that I actually found it). At the end it mentions two books by Sara Stein: *Noah's Garden*, about her own property, and *Restoring Noah's Garden*, about transforming a traditional garden into a natural habitat. I must go looking for them too.

6.

Bouquet Roses and Salt Beef

I HAVE TWO IDEAS that I have to pass along. Perhaps someone will try them before I get around to it and let me know how they work. The daughter of a friend is getting married in this month of brides and has chosen pink and cream roses for her bouquet. That reminded me of a tip I read a while back that was almost enough to make me want to be a bride again, but not quite. Maybe I should just go out and buy myself a dozen roses.

After the ceremony, cut the heads off the roses with a clean and very sharp knife like an X-acto, or a razor blade. Then make a sharp-angled cut through about 6 inches below. Slit the ends up about an inch and lightly score the bark around the slits. Immerse the slit and scored ends in a liquid or powdered rooting hormone, then set the cuttings in a pot of damp sterile potting soil or vermiculite. Mist with water, enclose in a plastic bag, and keep outdoors in a spot sheltered from midday sun. You have to keep misting several times a day, especially if it's very warm. The cuttings have no roots yet to take up moisture, so the misting is crucial. With any luck at all, you'll have roots within a month.

I say with any luck, not just because it seems a little far-fetched for some reason and not because I always think a bit of luck is involved with propagating new plants, but also because success with rose cuttings depends a lot on the parent plant and, of course, you won't know anything about that with roses from a florist's bouquet. The flowers on the new rose bushes may be quite different from the ones in your bouquet because the ones in the bouquet will probably have been grown on grafted rootstock. These new ones will be on their own roots, but the good news is that that will make them much hardier.

Even so, I wouldn't plant them out in the garden until next year. Grow them in pots the first season, winter them over in a frost-free place, and then plant them out to enjoy every summer of your married life. Now how romantic is that?

If the enticement of almost-free garden roses doesn't lead you down the garden path, how about creating your own designer garden path with the help of a 5-gallon bucket? Surely there's not a heart beating in a Newfoundlander anywhere that doesn't quicken at the thought of yet another use for that container we know so well as a vessel of salt beef and pork? Even those of us who don't even like salt meat and don't actually know how big a 5-gallon bucket is feel a sort of homey attachment to the very term.

There you are in Fort McMurray or Texas or Taiwan, and every time you set foot on your path of stylish stepping stones, you'll get a feeling of home because you cast those stones yourself using the bottom of a 5-gallon bucket as a mould. Just pour 2 inches of Ready-Mix, let set for a couple of hours, and then press in some aggregate stone or something to make an impression (beach pebbles, leaves, fern, a fir branch; how about doing one with a footprint each time friends or family visit?). Whether you use something from home or anything

from your new home, with a few inches cut from the bottom of a 5-gallon bucket, some concrete mix, and a little imagination, you can make your own stepping stones for a fraction of the price of store-bought ones. Let your stone cure for two or three days, misting to keep it from cracking, then gently turn it out.

I'll probably be at this one before I start propagating roses, and I think I'd spray the mould first to make the stone easier to turn out. Or maybe I'd just rub it with salt pork.

One Bag and One Dollar at a Time

IT'S ONE THING TO FIGURE out what to put where when you're creating a new garden, figuring out how to pay for all the things you're dreaming about can be enough to drive you straight to the hammock and a stiff drink. It is not for the faint-hearted.

By being bold and asking around, I found a source for soil on a semi-abandoned property just outside of town. The owner said, "Dig out behind the old barn where they used to dump the manure and help yourself." That was better to me than hearing "Will you marry me and help spend my riches?" (well, maybe) and that's just what I've been doing, filling dozens of doubled-up grocery store plastic bags with lovely old soil that must be just full of nutrients, lugging them back to town, and going back for more; six trips so far. A grocery bag of soil is nothing in a 30-foot trench.

Other people's gardens are an obvious source for plants, but you can only get so much from friends and family before they start hiding when they see you coming. Belonging to a garden club is a good idea, and another way is by scouting out private or fundraising plant sales. I found four last weekend; two in the Garage Sale section of my local paper, one in Community Happenings, and one in Articles for Sale.

I bought only perennials and only one of most of them because they're big enough to be divided into the plantings of three that work well for perennials.

Here's what I came home with: foxglove, columbine, monkshood, hollyhock, dwarf bleeding heart, shasta daisy, lavender, veronica, cornflower, calendula, saxifrage, sedum, gaillardia, butterfly bush, two different climbing honeysuckles, geranium, and Welsh poppy. That last one has me stumped. I can't find it in any of my books and, of course, the one disadvantage of buying this way is you can't always find the seller again to ask more questions.

But not to worry; surprises are part of the fun of gardening. I don't know what particular varieties I have of most of these. Down the road I will be much more particular about varieties and colours, but right now I'm just totally tickled to be able to get started with such a good collection of nice-sized perennial clumps, a small shrub, and two climbers for ... drum roll, please ... $25!

It's a good idea to write down the addresses and phone numbers of private gardeners who regularly sell plant divisions. They usually have everything potted up and ready to go at any time in the season, but don't keep advertising all summer long. Something growing in a pot can be successfully planted into your garden at any time, not just at the beginning of the season. It's not ideal, but I've never had any trouble. It's not so much being planted, but being dug up at the wrong time that plants don't like.

Now if I could only get two good weather days in a row to top up the bed along the wire fence, I could get them in the ground. I don't mind working in a little drizzle if it's warm, but single-digit temperatures, wind, and rain are not the stuff gin-and-tonic gardeners are made of.

Undaunted, I am going plant hunting again this weekend. A local Pathfinder's group has been smart enough to do up a plant list for their sale, so I am going to be in line for ajuga, bee balm, red lupins, black-eyed Susans, ivy, ribbon grass, rugosa roses, cosmos, and double red nasturtiums (the last two are annuals). I'm budgeting another whopping $25.

I need help in whipping the contents of my Whip-Pit into compost. I spin it around every day, but it isn't heating up. I imagine a manufactured model would come with some tips on various quantities and recommended ratios, while I'm pretty much doing what I'd do with a bin composter, throwing things in willy nilly. The tumbler has much less air exposure and maybe that's a problem; I may need to drill some holes in it.

I'm sure someone will help me with the finer points of compost tumblers and fill me in on Welsh poppies. Gardeners, shoestring and otherwise, stick together.

8.

Lasagna, Meconopsis, and Memories

THE FIRST TIME I HEARD of the lasagna method of making planting beds was from a freelance writer in a complimentary copy of a broadsheet-style publication called *The East Coast Gardener*, published in Dartmouth, NS. Right away I decided the writer, Carol Matthews of Yarmouth, NS, might just be my new best friend, and she didn't even know me. Sorry, Janine, but any woman who tells me how to turn grassy areas (grass and weeds and whatever green stuff growing does not a lawn make) into flower or vegetable areas in a day or two without breaking my back is practically a candidate for garden beatification in my book.

You spread the area you want converted from sod to garden bed with six or seven layers of newspapers, wetting them down as you go. This not only keeps them from blowing away, but helps them to decompose faster. On top of this you spread about 2 feet of topsoil, if you can afford that much. Right away you can plant annuals and small perennials and by next year, the newspaper has decomposed, along with the grassy turf beneath it, and you have another 6 inches or so of soil to work with.

I suppose you can also use various materials such as compost, grass clippings, leaves, rotted barn litter, old hay, horse manure, and eventually you'll have soil if you layer the right proportions of brown and green material, as if you were composting, which I guess you would be, and you'll have to wait longer to plant.

If you've ever gone through the sod-turning method of making new garden ground, you'll understand why I was so delighted to learn this, especially since I'm determined to eventually become mower-free.

Of course any sensible person would start with a small patch first, just to see how it works, but Carol says she's used this method in several locations and it always works well. That's good enough for me. A gardener would never make such a claim if it wasn't so.

I've been collecting newspapers like mad, and the only thing that will stop me from rushing out and covering the whole garden this year is that I can't afford to buy that much topsoil and can't face the challenge of getting enough quantities of compostable materials to do the whole thing. Why do even the simple pleasures have to involve money?

If I did have a supply of rich soil and could get the whole garden ready for planting, I wouldn't be able to afford that many plants. Even though I have to say I've done very well this year with all my bargain finds so far, spread over the back and front yards, they wouldn't go very far.

I'm also doing extremely well with e-mails from readers. Among other things I now know that Welsh poppy, *Meconopsis cambrica*, grows to about 10 inches, likes shade, has yellow or orange flowers, and self-seeds a little too heartily in some places; that the delicate flower is best planted where it can be admired close up; that it has a blue cousin, *Meconopsis papaveraceae*, and that a Macleaya poppy spread about 4 feet in one season in a South Shore Nova Scotian garden and that there is a Web site, women.com/homeandgarden, where you can get information and pictures on over 1,000 plants.

I also learned that you never know when you'll hear nice words from and about the past. Wow. Maybe I've been too harsh on this new technology stuff. I love getting e-mails from readers, but when Nova Scotia writers mention things like "garden by the sea" and "little island in Chester Basin," I want to be there.

I do miss Nova Scotia. I started writing there, made lifelong friends, and lost my heart there to a Cape Breton man whose garden potential I was not destined to learn, and now the only daughter I have on this continent, whom I haven't seen in months, is serving coffee at the Daily Grind in Halifax instead of coming home for the summer.

I'm having a sooky day. Blame it on all those e-mails from nice Nova Scotians stirring up memories. Now if only one would e-mail me about how to whip my Whip-Pit into shape.

9.

One Potato, Two Potato

A couple of weeks past the official date when it's considered safe to put out annuals, which is what most people were doing when we finally got a stretch of warm weather this week, and what was I doing? Planting potatoes. I suppose such aberrant behaviour doesn't surprise any of you who read my ramblings regularly, but it actually surprised me.

The last time I planted potatoes, fifteen or twenty years ago, I enlisted my father to help me harvest the crop. He made such fun of what he considered to be the paltry number of spuds that we dug up ("planting twenty pounds and digging ten") that it put me right off planting potatoes. I want whatever space I have for ornamentals anyway, but this year I have different considerations.

The opportunity has come up to rent my house for most of July and August for an enormous sum of money to a family wanting to come home from Japan for the summer and I just have to take it. The apartment is barely habitable as is, so I'm going to be spending my time visiting friends and family in Nova Scotia and northern Ontario, meeting as many gardeners as I can and picking up good gin-and-tonic tips. Of course I'll spend some of the rent money on the trip, but it will do my spirit good, and there'll still be enough left to keep the wolf away for another day or two.

On my budget I obviously cannot justify spending money on annuals that the people living here may not even look after. Then a friend offered me some excess red seed potatoes and the rest of my garden was planned. In fact, I'm so enthusiastic about the idea of little new potatoes that I rushed back to the store where I saw Yukon Gold seed some weeks ago, but of course it was all gone. Yukon Gold is the best-tasting potato I have ever eaten and I'm not taken in by labels such as "yellow-fleshed potato." They are seldom as good as the original Yukon Gold.

Yes, it's late to be planting potatoes. And no, I won't be around to do the hilling up and keep an eye on the watering. So what? Potatoes, like many root crops, are reasonably independent and lack of rain is seldom a problem in St. John's.

If I was looking for a yield of big fellows to keep me in Jigg's dinners through the winter months, I'd be out of luck, but a few weeks of tiny new potatoes will suit me just fine, and that I can be pretty well assured of, even after a six-week absence.

I used a planting tip relayed to me from an Irishman, which supposedly makes it a great tip. After you've cut your seed potatoes into sections, making sure they all have eyes, of course, let the cut edges become quite dry in the open air before you plant them. This will take a few days, depending on the weather. I guess it would be a good idea to cover them if it rains. I'm also not digging any of my very well-rotted manure into the potato bed because I remember that as a policy of old Newfoundland farmers.

This year I had my first Father's Day without a father. Do you think there could be something subliminal to the fact this is the year that I am once again trying potatoes in my garden? I will miss his teasing, and was almost tempted to forget the potatoes because of it, but life, and gardening, must go on.

Don't be surprised if you see me peering over your fence this summer. The wonderful thing about gardeners is that they never mind people stopping to take a look.

A Four-legged Lawn Mower Would Be Best

I AM NOT A DELICATE FLOWER in the garden. Never having been fortunate enough to find (or maybe smart enough to keep) a gardening man to tiptoe through the tulips with, I have become very self-sufficient. If a hole needs digging, I dig it, but I hate mowing.

One summer, in my first job as a professional gardener, at the Glynnmill Inn in Corner Brook, I moved 20 tons of topsoil in a wheelbarrow and climbed a ladder to the third floor to trim the Boston ivy away from the windows. I don't do heights well, but I wanted this job, so of course I didn't tell them that. I also didn't tell them I didn't know how to drive the company truck because it was a standard, or that I had never used a lawn mower.

That was one thing I decided early in my life with Former 'Usband. My aversion to all things mechanical was well known, but if F.U. had had just one hint that I was willing to master the lawn mower, I know what I would have been doing while he was busy arranging an early tee-off time.

Anyway, down at the hotel, I was ignoring the grass, hoping that maybe the maintenance guy would do it, but knowing the day of reckoning was coming. The mower was a gas machine and I couldn't for the life of me figure out how to get the thing started. Finally, I had to casually ask for help, making the excuse that I was used to an electric one.

I also learned to climb an extension ladder and cut ivy with my eyes closed; took the truck under the cover of darkness, in reverse all the way, to a deserted cul-de-sac, and practised changing gears and starting on a hill.

I lost 25 pounds that summer, but not my aversion to lawn mowers. Two non-functioning gas mowers came with the house I bought in Stephenville. I didn't get them fixed. I either hired a student on the "bring your own mower" plan, or there was a helpful swain around who knew the true way to my heart was to be handy.

Then, late last fall, a friend gave me an old-fashioned push mower, the perfect thing for me—no fancy technology, no noise, and a bit of exercise. I put it away to await its inaugural run this summer.

My nephew did the grass for me once this year, but last week it was my turn. Of course, once you've let the grass get too high, the only old-fashioned tool that will do the trick is a scythe. Not having one on hand, I realized I had to whipper-snip first.

I was loath to borrow one, knowing as soon as I touched it something would probably go wrong, but wanted to try using one before I bought one. Brother-in-Law said, "Take ours." Friend Mitchie said, "Ours is really easy to use."

It took two days, both whipper-snippers, four trips back and forth for advice, a trip to Canadian Tire, and the patience of Job to finish the job. After all that I was ready to crack, but it was done and the thought of being able to maintain my hated grass myself, without worrying about the workings of an engine, pleased me to no end.

So out came the push lawn mower this week. It didn't work. The push mower that has nothing to break down broke down. The wheels wouldn't go round. Something as basic as the wheel wouldn't work for me. I turned the thing upside down and laboriously cut a lot of stringy, grassy stuff from around where the wheels were attached to the body, which made it a bit better, but still no good really. There doesn't appear to be any rust, but I guess some oil and stuff is needed.

Either that or a goat.

To Each His Own

A FEW WEEKS AGO, I was bragging about the great variety of perennials I bought at yard sales; one of this, one of that, a couple of something else. What I neglected to point out was why I bought that way. One of any perennial makes absolutely no sense in a garden, so you know I would never do anything like that (ha) unless I had a good reason.

Well, I admit I do get carried away when I find anything for a dollar, but it's also a good idea if you're in a new environment, to try one plant in your garden first and see how it does before you plant more of it. St. John's is a different zone from Stephenville, my soil is different, and so is my sun, ergo I have excuses for not making decisions and committing myself to certain plants yet.

My vision for this garden, and I think the best plan for any garden, regardless of size, is to have drifts of things; large drifts in a large garden, small ones or clumps in a small garden. While I'm building toward that, I'll plant one of different things in what I think of as my holding bed. Then when I actually see its colour and shape, I'll have a better feel for where and if I want more of it in the garden.

Even things that I know well, like day lilies, have hundreds of different varieties, all with different shades, heights, and blooming periods, and I hope I never stop bringing home completely new things to try out.

Just this week, strolling around Parry Sound, Ontario, Baby Sister and I were taken by great clumps of bright yellow flowers in a few gardens. We both want them in our own gardens. I don't know what they were, and there was no one around to ask, but evening primrose popped into my mind, even though from a distance I couldn't be sure. Hopefully I'll be able to find out for sure before we leave the area. If not, I'll look them up when I get back home and if I'm wrong, the quest will be on.

I'm staying in a cottage with a garden. I phrase it that way because to use the term "cottage garden" would be misleading. It's beautiful and a perfect illustration of a garden being a very individual thing, and a reflection of the gardener. There is a lot of stonework and lawn, and yards and yards of

clipped cedar hedges. It was all done by our host and his father, who transplanted all the cedars from islands in Georgian Bay. So much work to create and now so much work to maintain, but they obviously love the sense of order they've created and probably think nothing of spending hours mowing and trimming.

There's yellow potentilla and periwinkle, some irises, and lots of yellow sedum that apparently grows wild here. First, I thought my host was mistaken about the sedum being wild, and that it must have naturalized from another garden, but this stuff is all over the place and I was wrong. I learn something new in every garden I visit.

A neat raised bed holds orderly rows of squash, lettuces, peppers, and tomatoes. Wire cages are in place, all ready to keep anything from sprawling. There are a few annuals, but this seems very much the garden of two men who want things to be nice, but don't bother much with new ideas.

It sort of makes me wish I could find me one of those—a strong man who likes working in the garden, but doesn't have a lot of ideas to conflict with mine. Early in my marriage, I had visions of working side by side in the garden with F.U. He knew absolutely nothing about gardening and had no interest in doing it, but didn't take much to the concept of simply doing things my way. After a few rackets, I learned not to ask him to help me.

Perhaps he was smarter than I thought.

A Rose is a Rose is the Making of a Gardener

TODAY I VISITED A GARDEN in Lively, Ontario, just outside of Sudbury, in zone 4. Grace, the wife of the gardening team, was remarking on having to divide perennials much sooner than she expected. Clumps of lamb's ears and goat's beard are outgrowing the ample space they were given.

There are lovely masses of creeping thymes, one of her favourites. Blue and white delphiniums, veronica, lamium, heuchera, coreopsis, and day lilies are only some of the species in this garden, carved into a slope down to Long Lake. So what's so unusual about that, you might well ask? The garden is only two years old, that's what, and looks like it's been there for years! Parts of it are only a year old, and even ordinary nursery material that was planted this spring has tripled in size.

And even though I know it's partly my own fault for being a gin-and-tonic gardener, I'm bemoaning that my garden doesn't grow like that. I'm consoling myself with the fact that I don't have a gardening partner. Not that that's a consolation—more of an excuse—but it does make a difference.

Grace and Ray are retired and have obviously put in two years of hard work in creating their lakeside haven. Ray, a Finn, says he does the heavy work, and gives Grace the credit for the ornamentals, but one element would be much less without the other.

Stone paths, low stone walls, and stone terraces provide the surroundings for beds shaped to the land. Throughout, white birches, native to the property, provide dappled sunlight and harmonize the non-natives with the land.

What's the secret? Not 20-20-20 or any other miracle fertilizer created by science. Grace is an organic gardener all the way. She uses compost, bone and blood meal, and digs shredded leaves into the soil.

"Ah ha," I thought. "They must have a compost tumbler because they haven't been here long enough to have made that much compost." I'm still desperately trying to find someone with a compost tumbler that really does make compost in two weeks so I can learn how to do it with mine and I thought maybe I'd struck black gold this time, but no, they use the old-fashioned, three-sided, double-bin method. In fact they had a tumbler and didn't like it. I don't know if that makes me feel worse or better about mine.

In the fall, Ray piles all the leaves from the property onto a big flat area, ending up with a mound about chest-high. Then he spends about four hours going around and around with the lawn mower until they're all ground up.

Back at my little spot down the lake, (a cozy fifth-wheel RV I've nicknamed The Garret belonging to and parked outside the house of my old friends, Renee and Jacques) they have approached their land differently. Stands of birches remain, but they frame grassy slopes from the house down to the lake, accented by two blue spruce trees and an airy pine.

Containers of annuals provide splashes of colour and window boxes adorn a little guest cottage tucked into the hill, and even a little storage shed. Where the land is steep, Jacques has built retaining walls for small kitchen gardens, and, like Grace and Ray's, they don't fight the land, but conform to it in irregular shapes. Both properties are lovely. In one, the beds demand most of the attention. In the other the lawn is king, but both share pride of ownership and respect for nature.

I sit lazily in the swing, dreaming what my property would look like if I lived here. Wilder than both of these I'm sure, but still sharing that same pride and respect for the land. Renee would admire my garden, but she wouldn't want it for herself, and that's just the way gardens should be. I'd have masses of shrub roses; she has one climber, and it's not doing very well because it doesn't get enough sun.

She says she's not a gardener, but she cares, and she's going to move it so it will climb over the sign that welcomes us at the top of the driveway. If that rose takes off, how long do you think it will be before she's gets another one? And another one. Sometimes that's how a gardener is born.

Water Grows Gardeners as Well as Gardens

MY FRIEND RENEE is flirting with danger. She who declares that with her golfing and her kayaking and her walking and her gym workouts and myriad other fitness activities, she doesn't have the time or interest to become a gardener, is about to cross over the line and she doesn't even know it yet.

It seems to have all started with a frog.

Before I got here, she had decided she wanted a little trickling fall of water on the patio, coming from the mouth of an iron frog, but she doesn't just want one of those tabletop models that simply (and very nicely) supply the soothing sound; she wants a water lily or two and some cattails. She jokes that this desire for the frog is because she is of the French-Canadian persuasion, but I know something that she doesn't.

This is the beginning of Renee becoming a water gardener. Serendipitously, she has found an element in gardening that appeals to her, even though she doesn't even consider it gardening yet.

She's started off with a set of four clay pots that we found on sale for one-third off. (This time of year, it's easy to find gardening things on sale; in fact, if it's not on sale, I wouldn't buy it.) These pots have a coppery glaze and an Aztec design and the largest is about 12 inches high and 12 inches in diameter.

She couldn't wait to start experimenting with how to arrange them when we got back to their house. Then nothing would do but Jacques had to get at the pump and start experimenting with the water flow patterns. The next morning when they returned from kayaking down the lake to meet a friend, what did all three of them come back with? You guessed it, water lily and iris roots.

But she's not interested in gardening! The only reason she took me to see a neighbour's pond is to provide me with column inspiration, saying, "You'll never get it from my garden." As if I was the only one who might get inspired!

The neighbours, Dianna and John, had a good thing and a bad thing happen to them last year. Their daughter decided she wanted to get married at the lake, a good thing, of course—a happy occasion; a bad thing because their garden apparently wasn't the stuff wedding dreams are made off; a good thing because they found a new landscape graduate to help them transform the garden into a setting fit for a bride.

Talk about a double whammy! A wedding and an instant garden could be enough to force a newly retired couple back to the chain gang, but the graduate was willing to give his first clients a good deal. Dianna and John already had begun water gardening, so they just had to speed up what they would have done eventually anyway.

Now they have two lovely ponds. The larger one was made freeform with a flexible liner; the smaller one with a rigid mould. The edges are concealed with local stone and a variety of flowering perennials. One has a natural stone cascade, the other a spout fountain. Koi and goldfish are flashes of gold between lilies from the lake. Frogs have moved in, and last year a garter snake took up residence. To the misfortune of some of the goldfish, so did a kingfisher, but so far this year he seems to have found a better neighbourhood.

Talk about inspiration. Renee and Jacques's kayaking friend, a transplanted Englishman who was also with us, started looking at the natural rock on his property and realizing how easily he could have the trickling water sound he loves. And I overheard Renee uttering those magic words: "We'll start small, but who knows?"

She's hooked. And hey, wait until she finds out what good exercise digging holes and lugging rocks can be.

Everything Including the Kitchen Sink

AUGUST 2000

I've personally always avoided water gardens—making them for myself, that is, not enjoying someone else's. I had this feeling that water gardens were complicated, I suppose, because they require a pump and I'd rather have my nails pulled than get involved with anything mechanical, electrical, or technical in any way.

Meet the braver, bolder me, ready to go where no Amish wannabe has gone before. If nothing else (and there is lots else) my visit to northern Ontario these past few weeks has made my fears of water gardening seem totally irrational.

Renee feels about gardens like I do about hairdos; we have to have one; we'd like it to be attractive, but if that means doing anything complicated, we'll settle for just not being too ugly. Now, with just a set of clay nesting pots, an iron frog, and a small pump, even Renee has a water garden.

Suddenly, seeing the simplicity of it all (not to mention the shame of Renee being able to do what I've been intimidated by) I can't wait to get home and start my own. That old porcelain sink/drain board combination I've been saving for just such inspiration could be the beginning. I've always pictured it covered with moss, catching trickling water in its tiny basin. Now my imagination has gone totally to wing again, and I have visions of cascades and miniature falls. Solid rock, which I've always thought of as a detriment to gardening, now seems like a wonderful commodity, and I'm almost wishing I had more of it—almost but not quite.

I think that's the Newfoundlander in me. Not that in spite of the misnomer "the Rock" we don't have our share of fertile growing areas, but we've long learned to adapt to any soil conditions, and to make creative use of whatever we have on hand and we do have some magnificent rock. With a simple pump, a water supply, and a little imagination, a stone outcrop can be transformed into a breathtaking trickling wall because there is simply no terrain that cannot be turned into a garden, including solid rock.

Alpines will cling happily to small indentations; deeper pockets can be hollowed out and filled with soil for larger species, or to form small cascading pools with marginal aquatics (that's garden-speak for plants that must have their roots wet, but their growth above water).

I know this only because as soon as I got bitten by the water-gardening bug, I went off to the bookstore to educate myself. I bought Time Life's *Easy Water Gardens* by Alison R. Francis, a great beginner's book. It shows you how to use everything from an old galvanized pail to a pile of beach rocks to an old rubber tire to create an interesting water feature for your garden.

Of course it shows the fancy stuff too, and has lots of simply explained and illustrated information on liners and plants and lighting, but, well, it's the lure of the silk purse that turns me on. Turning pigs' ears, such as too much rock or a cast-off container, into something alive and beautiful tickles me pink.

Like I said, that's the Newfoundlander in me. And that's a good thing.

Absence Makes the Bushes Grow Higher

THE FOLLY OF NOT REMOVING STUMPS! Back from my wanderings in other gardens, I couldn't wait to wander my own and see how all the stuff I planted along the back fence had done, and what changes might have taken place in the six weeks I was away.

It was very late when I arrived, and I was knackered, so I contented myself with a look out the back porch window. I could make out lots of promising vegetation along the fence, including two huge clumps easily up to my chin. Not having planted any shrubs in those particular spots, I went to bed wondering which of my perennials had taken off so well. Probably the bee balm, I thought, as I drifted off to dreams of majestic spires of delphinium and glorious drifts of black-eyed Susans.

Today is another day. I can't even find the bee balm. A few things are almost as high as an elephant's eye; the grass and not the ornamental kind, the potatoes, a lovely cluster of sweet rockets I didn't even plant, a maple bush, and a black ash bush. Bushes apparently are what you get when you make a bed around last year's tree stumps instead of removing them; new tree sprouts come out all over the stumps and make a bush/tree!

The "bushes" are not unattractive, especially the ash, but they obliterate everything I planted around them. They haven't, however, discouraged a native morning glory or bindweed (*Convolvulacea sepium*) from competing in the takeover attempt. It reminds me of some wry old advice; if you're having your first spring in a new garden and aren't sure how to tell the weeds from the perennials, just pull up everything and the ones that come back are weeds.

The seeds for the bindweed may have been in the soil from behind the old barn and/or the manure I used because it's everywhere. There was no sign of it behind the barn and the manure was well rotted and dry, at least two years old, so that will tell you how long some seeds stay potent. Of course, none of the packets I had from last year germinated, but such is the perversity of nature.

Monkshood, mallow, harebells, perennial geranium, and

calendula are blooming. The feverfew seems to be finished, but deadheading may encourage a second round. Virginia creeper has gotten a tiny hold on the wire fence, but my quick search on this wet day didn't even find either of the honeysuckle. It's probably under the morning glory, dead or alive.

One of my verandah pots has a lovely bushy rose, about 18 inches high, with very small leaves and lots of buds. That was a mystery until I remembered the little 6-inch miniature I bought at the supermarket around Easter for about $6. It was covered in buds, then bloomed for weeks with a sweet apricot-tinged red flower. Finally it stopped and the leaves turned yellow and fell off.

I cut it back, stuck it in an outdoor pot, and forgot about it. It's now three times as big. When it finishes blooming again, I'll try bringing it in to the basement, cutting it back and letting it rest for a few months, try to remember to water it occasionally, and bring it out again around February. These things often get treated like throwaways and I'm so proud of myself when I keep them going.

I'll have to wait until the wet spell passes before I really check everything out. There was a time when I would have hauled on the rainsuit and mucked in right away, but that was before I adapted the gin-and-tonic gardening philosophy.

The Englishman I met while I was away is arriving next week so while I wait for the garden to dry out, I'm concentrating on spiffing up the verandah, which I didn't do before because I was going away. Having to have the roof torn off the verandah after it almost collapsed kind of took away from the ambiance anyway.

But now, the wicker is all set out, rocking chairs and mats are in place, and I'm off to find some great container bargains. My verandah will be charming even if it doesn't have a roof.

16.

Sizing Up the Future

THIS IS A GREAT TIME of the year to be looking for bargains, not just for the future, but for the rest of this season. I found pots with two luscious begonias each, marked down to $2.50 a pot; geraniums and New Guinea impatiens for 99¢; and the largest, healthiest black-eyed Susan vine (*Thunbergia*) I've ever seen for only $8.

Baby Sister's front bed was looking a little sad in places, and six pots of those begonias brightened it up no end. For $15, who cares if the season is winding down? She'll still get another six weeks of pleasure out of those begonias, and could lift the tubers and save them for next year but I know she won't.

This is also a good time of year for driving around, sizing up what charms you about other people's gardens. That doesn't just mean look at gardens that look great; around here lots of gardens will look great in mid-August, but look past the overall picture and really pay attention to what appeals most to you.

I've been noticing day lilies, shasta daisies, mallow, and climbing roses. In many gardens the Oriental and Asiatic lilies are absolutely gorgeous, blazing with bright, startling colour, but I've realized that I don't really like being startled in the garden. Other lilies catch the eye and last a long time, but just don't call to me like the airy day lilies swaying above satiny green swords.

Shasta daisies can fool you; they're perennial, but they often die out after a few years. Sometimes they reseed, sometimes they don't. To me they're comfort flowers; a clump of daisies will coax a smile from my spirit on the darkest day. They look so determined to stand upright and be cheerful. That sort of stiffness and determination can get on your nerves sometimes in people, but somehow shasta daisies can get away with it.

The mallow, on the other hand, always seems to be just a little languid, like some Victorian lady with the vapours. It's always in a soft tangle of feathery green with pale pink-and-white blossom cups that seem barely capable of capturing a drop of dew, yet it's really tough, remaining steadfast year after year. I like that.

I've also realized that there is almost nothing in any garden that I wouldn't sacrifice for a climbing rose in full bloom, including the huge maple in my backyard. I think I'll delve into the trauma of trees more next week.

In my bargain shopping I did see perennials at half-price, but I must visit a few more places before I decide what to get. Some of the above, I hope, but first I have to get cracking and get more ground ready.

This is, in a way, the most important gardening time for me this year. The weather is much nicer for working outdoors than it was in spring; I have more time; almost everything is on sale. I've still got stacks of newspapers ready to try the no-sod-turning method of turning lawn into garden. The Englishman is visiting, so it's perfect timing to find out if he's really made of gardening stuff or if it was all just a ruse to impress me. As if it was that easy!

A Tree by Any Other Name Might Smell Sweeter

LET'S TALK REALISTICALLY about trees in a garden. You have to be so careful when you suggest taking one down; in some company you might as well confess to being an axe murderer. But sometimes there are good things and bad things about particular trees. What you have to do is make two lists and add them up.

I'm looking through the branches of that huge maple right now. My desk is two storeys up, three, actually, if you consider that most of the basement is totally above ground. As I sit here and work, I'd rather look at a lovely network of branches and leaves than at the cul-de-sac behind it, so that's a good thing about the maple. This tree also shades my dormer office from the heat of the midday sun. That's a good thing in summer, and I suppose a good thing in winter, when even the bare branches provide some windbreak.

That's the end of the good things.

Now for the other side of the ledger: The roots of this maple take a lot of nourishment and moisture from the soil. That's not a good thing. It provides a lot of shade on the deck, which is also not a good thing when you yearn for a bit of sun on your body and love sun-loving plants for containers. It ensures that my garden is suitable for many shade-loving species, but not many of the things that I crave, especially the old-fashioned roses, which is definitely a bad thing, and from any other vantage point except my garret, it provides no privacy from the cul-de-sac and hinders the planting of the lower canopied trees and high shrubs that would give me lots of privacy when I'm actually in the garden—another minus.

Intellectually I feel tree-hugging should boil down to the right trees in the right place. In my backyard I could be downright affectionate to one of the low-branching flowering crabapples like Sargenti, or a weeping Japanese maple. Even a 20-foot Paul's Scarlet hawthorn would be short compared to my giant maple and wouldn't shade nearly as much of the garden. But my emotions have always waged a strong war with my intellect and have won more often than I care to admit, and taking down a majestic tree is hard to do no matter how much you wish it would just go away.

Brother-in-Law has just taken down a big tree in his backyard because of the same problem—too much shade, and too high a canopy to provide any privacy from the neighbouring deck. They still have some lovely trees, but 8- to 12-foot high shrubs are what they (and I) really need for privacy. Some shrubs will grow happily under the umbrella of a large maple, but if you want sun-lovers in a relatively small garden, you have to make some tough choices.

Some of my old favourites, like Pee Gee hydrangea and mock orange, aren't fussy about a lot of sun, but others, like lilacs and forsythia and quince and almost anything that flowers, and most definitely roses, prefer the sun and that's all there is to it.

So what to do? I haven't really gotten a handle on the mess from the trees I took down last year. It almost boggles the mind to start again. Plus I can't help but be repulsed by the idea of killing a tree that was here first and has been living much longer than I have. Part of me thinks, "What right do I have to do such a thing?" but then part of me yearns for the climbing roses I see in other sunnier gardens.

There's no point in suggesting the front of the house, which is a northern exposure. The downhill side is a possibility, but not ideal. Even if I can establish shade-tolerant vines to screen the back fence and view, that still won't solve the problem of no sun on the deck.

The only easy solution is to pay attention to all these things before you buy a house, but it's obviously too late for that.

What would Martha do, I wonder?

Mighty Maple/Mighty Miniature

SEPTEMBER 2000

I knew I'd get mail if I wrote about cutting down a big tree, but I thought at least one rose lover would say, "Yes, my dear, if you want roses, there is no other way." I guess rose lovers aren't as communicative as tree lovers. Anyway, it worked. You've all got me feeling guilty about planning to take down that maple.

Everybody says thinning is the answer. I just can't picture how it would look thinned to the point where enough sun would come through to keep me and a rose garden happy, but Sheri writes that a good arborist is the answer.

Donna, bless her, didn't move me a bit when she wrote about how useful trees are for hammocks and bird feeders because I don't use this particular one in those ways, but then, darn her, she just had to remind me of the sounds of rustling leaves and the shelter the branches give the birds who come to my feeders elsewhere in the garden.

I am so easily swayed. And I have remembered something else mildly encouraging. One of the stars of my garden this year is that miniature rose I bought in bloom at the supermarket for Easter. When I transplanted it into a pot on the deck in June, it was downright sad. All the leaves were yellow and dropping and there wasn't a bloom in sight. Right now it has sixteen buds and flowers. It does not get good sun, has never been fed, and probably dried out more than a few times while I was away.

I'm so impressed with it that maybe I'll even take some cuttings so I'll have more next year. My rose book says early fall is the best time to try this and that because miniatures grow on their own roots, cutting will come true to the parent.

You select shoots about 4 inches long from this year's growth. Trim to one leaf bud, dip the end in rooting hormone, and plant firmly in a container of good potting soil. When new growth appears, pot them up separately. By spring they should be ready to bloom and/or set outside.

The operative word here for me is "should," but it's worth a try. Also I don't see anything in my book that says miniature roses are less fussy than other types. In fact, just the contrary, so maybe I'm worrying too much about not having the ideal conditions for the shrub roses I love. I could try one or two before I do anything drastic with the maple, which is a logical plan since one or two are all I can afford to start with anyway, and the very cost of taking down the maple breaks my heart.

But back to care of miniatures. I talked about bringing mine indoors and keeping it for next year by pruning them back, giving them a rest in an unheated room until February, and then bringing them into the warmth again, but apparently if you keep them on a tray of wet pebbles with a fluorescent light above them, you can get blooms every two months all year round. My book explains that British and U.S. rose enthusiasts differ on whether to treat miniatures as true houseplants or not.

As neither of the above, I guess Canadians can do whatever they feel like.

Desperate for Company

I HAVE A YOUNG FRIEND who has a pet worm. I myself have always preferred the kind of pet that gives back to me what I give to it, affection and company. I suppose it's only a step to draw some human analogies from that even though I've yearned often enough to meet a man who would be good in the garden (I thought I might have found him in the Englishman but there's more to life than gardening) that you'd think I'd have no doubts about pets that would help me out in the garden.

Well, maybe pets is not quite the right word, and why I'm bringing the male reference into a column about worms doesn't bear thinking about, but worms it is. I've been reading about worm composting, or vermicomposting as it is known to those who have friendly relations with thousands of worms.

Yep, thousands. I think that's what's making me squeamish. I finally got to see a real live indoor worm composter in a large plastic storage bin and, of course, got all excited about the idea of making compost in the house all winter. For a few minutes there, a worm seemed like an ideal pet: You feed it kitchen scraps; you never have to walk it or clean up after it; it doesn't bark or shed; you can leave it alone for extended periods of time. And in return for this benign neglect, it makes compost for you.

Okay, so it wouldn't keep your feet warm on a cold night, or run to meet you at the door, and you wouldn't have much fun playing with it unless you took it fishing, but all in all, a fairly rewarding creature to have around. Except that one or two aren't much good. In fact, if your kitchen produces 1 pound of compostable scraps a day, you need about 2,000 worms.

If you can get over the mental picture of that, this worm composting could be the best thing since sliced bread, but you can't feed them sliced bread. Give them basically the same things you'd use in regular compost, i.e., vegetable and fruit peelings, tea bags, coffee grounds, and crushed eggshells.

But I'm getting ahead of myself and my worms. I took down some worm Web sites and set out to enlighten myself on worm husbandry. (There's the man reference again and I didn't coin that word.)

First you choose a container about 8 inches to a foot deep. Some people prefer wooden boxes or old drawers to plastic because the finished compost isn't as wet. It has to have lots of holes in the bottom for drainage and in the top for ventilation. Raise the container off the ground a few inches and place something underneath to catch excess liquid (use it for watering).

Then you have to provide the little wigglers with bedding to live in while they're busy converting your garbage to black gold. This can be shredded newspaper or chopped-up cardboard, fall leaves, straw, seaweed, sawdust, peat moss, compost, aged manure, or any combination—the more varied, the better for the worms. Fill the bin three-quarters full of this stuff and throw in a shovelful of sand to aid their little digestive tracts. All this should be moistened to wet-sponge consistency before you put it in the bin, and then loosened up to provide air pockets and easy movement. Then, and only then, is this castle fit for a kingdom of worms. And not just any worms.

Night crawlers and dew worms are not likely to survive. Red wigglers or manure worms are the best. Don't ask me what a manure worm is. Just check out your friendly neighbourhood manure pile and maybe you'll find out.

Who knew there was such a variety of worms? On the off chance that you don't have any horses or cows within sniffing distance, check your local worm suppliers. And believe it or not, there are too many worm Web sites to list here; www.wormdigest.org has lots of tips to get you started.

Sage Advice

I'VE BEEN GIVEN SOME THYME, garlic, chives, comfrey, and lovage. Some sages say dig and transplant in the spring and some say in the fall. I say it depends on where you are and when in the spring and fall. In the North trees and shrubs prefer to be moved in the early spring before they break dormancy because waiting until after they're dormant in the fall won't give the roots enough time to re-establish before winter, but if you have to move it or lose it, any time is worth a try. No one suggests August for transplanting anything not growing in a container (but August is the time to plant perennial seeds for next year).

My new specimens don't seem any the worse for being dug up and stuffed in plastic bags. The lovage and comfrey have been cut back. I'm not sure I even want them because I don't think I'll use them as herbs and the comfrey can get carried away, but it did get me thinking about maybe starting an herb garden.

I've always been sort of interested in herbs, but didn't have an easy one-book reference for how to use many of them. I know the bookstores have them, but on my budget I have to wait until it comes out in yard sale, never mind paperback. Even the library is no help because you have to bring their books back and what's the use of that on a Tuesday night when someone gives you a bunch of sage to strengthen your memory, but you can't remember how you're supposed to take it?

Anyway, last week I found an old herb book at a yard sale for seventy-five cents that tells you everything you ever wanted to know but were too shy to ask about every herb you ever heard of. Now I'm all set. And have I learned a lot, like how I have managed these many years without angelica I'll never know. The candied stems of this tall, dark, and handsome background plant will cause a disgust for alcoholic liquors, it will dispel lust in young persons, and the aroma of angelica will drive away serpents if it is charcoal-broiled.

And I'll bet you thought the best thing you could do with basil was make pesto. If it's in short supply, I'd say forget eating it and do your weight-struggling friends a favour: "A sprig placed under a woman's plate without her knowledge will curb her appetite." Obviously it won't

work if I place some under my own plate, so hopefully someone near to me will read this and come to my assistance.

And let's not forget chervil: "If the roots be boiled and dressed as the cunning cook knoweth, it will comfort the hearts of old people who feel dull and without courage, and will increase their lust and strength." I should get me some of that, but I guess I'm not as cunning as I could be because while the boiling part seems fairly simple, there could be many ways to dress a chervil root. I'm cunning enough not to be digging in the attic for Barbie clothes, but are we talking vinaigrette here or mayonnaise? It could be important.

And if, like me, you've haven't been growing herbs because full sun is generally recommended, don't despair. There are some—angelica, bee balm, chervil, comfrey, lemon balm, and French tarragon—that will grow well in partial shade. And if you do despair, try some of that lemon balm: "cordial and exhilarating ... powerfully chasing away melancholy."

The Knee Bone's Connected to the Thigh Bone

SOMETIMES IT'S REALLY HARD being a gardener and an impoverished struggling writer at the same time. It wouldn't be hard if the garden had been even partly established, but I have so much to do (and such dreams) that I really need to spend a bit of money on it right now, but I'm so frugal that I cannot waste money by putting the cart before the horse. In this case the cart is the garden and the horse is the house, which I'm starting to fear I may not even own come spring because the bank is being agonizingly bank-like in approving the funds I requested to create the apartment I need to make the whole thing work.

In the meantime I have a back porch chock full of newspapers waiting to turn sod into soil for next spring. Aside from having no money for topsoil, the newspapers have to be wetted down as you work and I have no hose outside. That's right, I water with a watering can, when I water at all, which is mainly spot watering new transplants.

The contractor has already said he'd put in some outside faucets while he's here doing the work on the apartment, which I expected would have started weeks ago except that nothing in renovating (and banks) ever seems to happen like you expect it to. Now that I've jumped through all the planning hoops and groveled and practically cried, "they" say it will all be approved, that I just have to have patience, but patience is not one of my myriad virtues and at least the garden helps keep my mind off my troubles.

The weather is wonderful—my favourite sunny-but-not-hot days. The birds that didn't need me all summer are back. This morning, I'm writing on Damian at the kitchen table so I won't miss any of the up-close action at the kitchen window feeders, and over breakfast, I dug out a favourite cottage garden article from a 1998 magazine just to encourage me and keep the devil out of my mind regarding the bank and the worry about maybe not getting the refinancing approved.

I shouldn't have done that because now I am itching to be out there worse than ever, puttering away toward the glorious profusion and organized confusion that is the cottage-garden style. Organized confusion reminds me of the bank again and I want to forget about that.

"Profusion" is a key word in the centuries-old cottage garden. Hard-working cottagers believed in getting use out of every inch of the small spaces they had. The vegetables, herbs, and small fruits that were so essential to their bodies also had to make room for the flowers that fed their spirits.

Front gardens were usually small, enclosed by fence or stone wall or hedge, and overflowing with plantings. My magazine tells me that in 1870, an American named Frank J. Scott decreed in *The Art of Beautifying Suburban Home Grounds* that the walled-off gardens of England were "rude-mannered" and that an open landscape with one lawn flowing into another was more democratic and American.

By the 1920s, many American garden writers actually declared not having a lawn to be unpatriotic and un-American. Thank goodness that madness never completely spread this far northeast, but the idea of lawn being an automatic must, unfortunately, caught on. I say unfortunately because to me, a person tending flowers in a garden appears much more approachable than a person mowing a lawn.

And I quite love fences. To me they don't mean "keep out." They simply mean "this is a separate garden room." Attractive sections of fence, wall, or hedge entice you to see what's on the other side, just as paths encourage you to wander.

It will be a while before I can do a fence out front, if ever, but I can't let myself think that so I am building imaginary fences instead. My heart wavers between traditional English picket and unpeeled spruce that is more characteristic of this area. I'm leaning toward the latter, but by the time I can afford it, who knows?

I think I'll go out and get some bulbs to plant. My spirit needs feeding more than my belly and there's nothing more hopeful than planting spring bulbs.

22.

The Bulbs Brought Me Luck

OCTOBER 2000

Three exciting garden things have happened to me this week. First, the bank finally took pity on me and approved the funds to do my downstairs renovations, so long before spring, my dream garden flat will be a reality, allowing me to live rent free while upstairs tenants pay my mortgage and enable me to keep my house and therefore my garden.

Second, in the spring I'm going to be doing a pilot for a *Gin-and-Tonic Gardener* TV series for CBC. Even if it doesn't get picked up, I'll have a bit more money to spend on my dream garden.

And third, maybe I'll have a gardening buddy close by. I've noticed that the front lawn of a house a few doors down was being dug up, but never did happen to pass by while the gardener was there until today, when I spied a woman about my age shaking out sods.

Of course I had to stop and ask her what she was planning to plant there. With a friendly smile and an interesting accent, she said flowers and vegetables, immediately adding that she didn't see why you couldn't grow vegetables in the front garden. As if she needed to defend such a strange notion to me, but of course she didn't know that because I haven't started getting rid of all my grass yet.

I didn't have much time to chat, but just the knowledge that I may have a gardening buddy down the street delights me to no end. Gardening, like many of life's pleasures, is better when it's shared. Of course other people on my street look after their gardens too, but somehow I got the feeling that this woman and I might have more in common. She remembered that I came to her yard sale when she moved in last year, but I haven't seen her since. Like me, I guess she had to do inside stuff first.

Now that my ship seems to be starting to move in a teeeeeeny bit from the horizon, I might even be able to afford topsoil to start making

my lasagna-method garden from sod, and I'm so optimistic that I think I'll plant a few more bulbs to celebrate.

As much as I enjoy looking at tulips and daffodils in other people's gardens, I'm interested in certain smaller bulbs for naturalizing around and throughout the perennials. I want a gentler, softer feel than you get with the taller traditional bulbs like the Darwin tulips and the King Alfred daffodils and because my garden is still in its infancy, I don't really have enough perennials yet to hide the foliage of these taller varieties once it starts to decay, and to me that is essential.

I think I'll start with the two types of scilla—siberica (Siberian squill) and campanulata (wood hyacinths). The squill is a wonderful vibrant blue, and can handle some shade, even though it blooms before most trees leaf out. The wood hyacinth is taller, blooms later, comes in pink, white, and blue and also does well in partial shade.

I may weaken and add some small narcissus like the 6-inch-high Tête-à-Tête or the 8-inch-high Minnow, but I'm more inclined to spend whatever I can afford just on the two scilla because more is definitely better when it comes to small bulbs, but bigger is better still, so always choose size over quantity with bulbs.

The squill is wonderful for naturalizing right in the lawn, but, of course, eventually I don't intend to have any lawn, so I'll put them and the others, with some bone meal, around the lilac tree and in among the perennials along the back fence.

Then as they increase I can move clumps to other parts of the garden. There's that optimism again!

There's Such a Thing as Too Tidy

IT'S NOT UNUSUAL for a gin-and-tonic gardener to find winter has arrived and a few garden chores just didn't get done. If it's been a really bad fall, I blame it on the weather because it's too cold/wet/just plain miserable to want to be out in the garden. If it's been a lovely fall I blame it on the weather because I get lulled into thinking there's lots of time; my metabolism kind of slows down and I dreamily enjoy the colours changing, the migratory birds, and that sweet sharpness in the air that makes fall my favourite season (tied for that honour with spring, when it all happens in the reverse).

In other words, I'm a procrastinator. The good news is that in gardening that's not always a bad thing. I used to feel like sort of a slovenly gardener because I rarely got around to cutting back the perennials in the fall. I never did cut back roses until spring, but among expert gardeners, there were always two trains of thought about this.

The conventional, older wisdom was that fall pruning was the thing to do. First of all, it tidied everything up and god knew any gardener worth her/his salt had to be tidy! Getting rid of dying stalks and foliage was also thought to cut down on the possibility of diseases and pests getting into your plants.

The other completely opposite expert advice was to do the minimum of tidying up and leave everything as is until spring because the old stalks and foliage actually provided the plant some winter protection and having fresh cuts in the fall would make the plant more susceptible to disease and pests.

Because I was never turned on by neatness in a garden, and because I am at my most gardening-enthusiastic in the spring (sap rising, metabolism quickening, spring fever, and all that stuff), I naturally choose to believe the latter. And the trend certainly seems to have come my way. So even if you're tempted by a mild spell to get out there and prune, you should lie down 'til the feeling goes away. Or get out there and do something else, like hill up roses and cover them and tender perennials with evergreen boughs. But then there are the experts who say don't do that until after the ground is frozen. Sometimes that doesn't even happen here, so you see what I mean; it all depends on whose advice you choose to pay attention to.

Many shrubs bloom on last year's growth, so you could prune away some or all of your flowers; ditto with spring bloomers. It is also generally agreed that in a cold climate it's better if you don't prune roses in the fall. If you do and have a mild spell, they may start new growth and mature canes have a much better chance against winter than tender new shoots. (That's also why you shouldn't fertilize them after July.)

Not pruning also means more surface exposed to damage from harsh, drying winds. Wrapping them in burlap is a good idea. Better still, make a cone around them with burlap and stakes or chicken wire and fill the cone with leaves or boughs or even soil. The ideal time to do this (and to mulch with boughs) is after the ground has frozen because it's not the freezing that hurts hardy shrubs and perennials, but the freezing/thawing that continually takes place in a variable winter. Of course you may get snow before the ground freezes, but you can do it if you lose the snow cover at anytime during the winter; better late than never is the rule for minimizing the freeze/thaw effects.

Aside from what's good for the plants, people are paying a lot more attention to the aesthetics of the winter garden than they used to, which makes sense considering how much winter some of us have. I want to see beauty whenever I look out the window, even if it is twenty below. Clumps and stalks and seed heads add more interesting shapes to a snowfall than levelled beds, especially if they've been planted with an eye to winter composition.

In my new and changing garden, I have no idea what I'll see this winter, but it does give me a little something to look forward to until next season.

24.

Digging Out/ Starting Again

MAY 2001

It's been a long hard winter of renovations, reservations, stymied expectations, and snow devastation and it's not over yet, but I don't care; I'm so happy to be a gardener again!

During the last week in April the winter from hell finally released my backyard. For weeks I was out there, every reasonably fine day, hacking at ice and shovelling away snow, doing what my mother used to call "rushing the season," except in this case it was more like dragging the season, kicking and screaming, because the season just didn't want to come.

When the snow finally melted, the sights in my poor backyard were enough to make me cry. I didn't exactly forget what got buried out there last fall and winter while I was tearing out walls in my basement. I just didn't realize how much. To say I didn't have the experience of seeing a winter garden take shape like I was looking forward to is an understatement.

It's all my fault. You know, I couldn't let any of the old lumber go to the dump, and me with a sweet little wood stove. Then I had some ridiculous idea of making a potato barrel out of one of two old oil drums, but can't for the life of me remember what I was going to do with the other one (not attempt to turn it into a compost tumbler, I'm sure).

They're out there, ugly and rusty and staring me in the face every time I go out the door. So is a huge mess of dirty old lumber, doors, and even a 100-year-old wire bedspring. Surely even I, in the depths of winter madness, couldn't have had envisaged that as a garden sculpture or trellis. Maybe I just gave up after realizing that a giant snow-and-lumber monster was growing out there.

Anyway, I did what any good Newfoundland woman would do. I used some of the lumber to hammer together a sawhorse and dug out my little bucksaw to saw up the firewood. I quickly realized that if I wanted to get that mess cleaned up and start gardening in earnest before the snow comes again next year, I was going to have to learn to use a chainsaw or wait for M.G. to visit.

M.G. is a good guy and a good friend from Stephenville days. He's like feverfew (*Maticaria*)—extremely persistent, not easily daunted, and too nice to eradicate.

I have my moments when the sheer simplicity of just letting feverfew take over completely is very appealing, but they don't seem to last. However, M.G. is due for a visit this weekend and will throw his chainsaw aboard with the slightest hint of wood to cut.

So I turned my attention to how my poor shrubs survived the record 27 feet of snow. Now I'm thankful that I've been too busy inside the house to put a lot of money into shrubs.

The perennials that I can see so far seem to be just fine, and why not? All that snow cover certainly protected them from the freezing/thawing damage that can occur in a normal St. John's winter. My few shrubs weren't so lucky. The cotoneaster and the viburnum I planted for the birds spent the winter where no bird would ever find them and look like they'd been attacked by an axe murderer. Ditto the burning bush out front, but the lilac and firethorn along the fence don't seem to have suffered much.

It's important to prune damaged parts as soon as possible because the plant will put all its energy into trying to heal the broken parts. If the overall shape isn't ruined, cut the damaged parts off with an angular cut just above an outward facing bud. Older specimens will likely benefit from a hard pruning. The rule of thumb for rejuvenating an old neglected shrub is to do it over three years, taking out a third of the old wood and cutting the rest back by a third each year, so maybe you can work that in to your damage repair if you're lucky enough to have old shrubs.

It is possible to simply mend some breaks, especially if you catch them before they start to dry out. Fit them back together just like you were mending a broken bone. You don't need to put anything on the wound, just wrap it well. I've seen them heal and flower in the same season wrapped in electrical tape, but the best thing to use is some kind of medical tape because it breathes.

If the damaged speciman reminds you too much of a Charlie Brown tree, I'd cut the whole thing back as far as it takes to come up with a reasonable shape. What have you got to lose? This year's flowers maybe, but next year it might even be better than ever. And think how proud you'll be!

Even if you have something like a flowering crab or dwarf fruit tree that has cracked right off, you don't have to give up yet. You could try espaliering it. (God, I'm ambitious in the spring!) Espalier is the method of training a plant to grow flat on a wall or fence either in a random pattern or in a design. Some methods actually tell you to start by taking out the main leader and letting side ones develop, so, again, what have you got to lose? Well, a bit of time and garden space, but it's worth a try and it might be fabulous.

. . . .

2 5 .

. . . .

Attracting Fairies

AMAZINGLY, THE MESS IS GONE, but of course I have to find another thorn in my side. When I look out, as I do so often, to enjoy whatever is happening in the garden, my eyes are inevitably drawn to the cul-de-sac behind my backyard and I really don't like it. It's not that the view of the street and the children who play there is unpleasant. I just want a more enclosed feeling here. In rural gardens we have wide-open spaces. In the city, cocooning is more my style, and you can't wrap yourself in a cocoon made of wire fence, which is what a previous owner installed.

I've had two years of fence sitting (please pardon the bad pun) with intimidation/indecision about what to do with the big shade trees along there. All have now been removed except for the biggest one, the Norway maple that has been high-pruned a bit to let in some more light. I'd like to prune up to about 20 feet, but I'm worried that the tree might look odd and still can't seem to make up my mind.

There was one lopsided specimen that I hesitated to take down because it held up the clothesline. Then at some point the light dawned that there's no law saying you have to cut down the *whole* tree, so I now have an 8-foot clothesline pole firmly rooted in the ground.

The two yard sale honeysuckles from last year seem to be still alive and offer some hope, but I think I'm giving up on the Virginia creeper that's now in its third year and really hasn't moved much. It's under the maple, so maybe the combination of shade and greedy roots are too much competition, so I'm going to move it further up the bank. The tiny yard sale bittersweet I planted last year didn't make it through the winter, but I think I'll try to find a sturdy nursery one because I love the look of the fall berries.

I've wired on some pieces of lattice for instant illusion of privacy and will keep planting whatever big healthy perennial climbers catch my fancy. I'll keep the ones that seem happiest right where they are and next

year move the others to any of a dozen bare spots around the house, deck, verandah, retaining walls, wherever. Ivy, wisteria, hydrangea, clematis, hops, silver lace, grape; there are lots to choose from.

It's all trial and error no matter how much you read or experience about gardening. I was sure that Virginia creeper would clamber over that fence in no time. The firethorn nearby came through the winter, but is also in the third year and really hasn't grown at all, so maybe I should try to find it a better home too.

I was picturing a pillar rose covering the tall tree stump/clothesline until I realized how impossible it would be to dig a good hole through the tree roots. I've decided to use it to support different annual climbers: sweet peas, nasturtiums, morning glory, black-eyed Susan vine, not to mention scarlet runner beans and all the other climbing veggies and gourds, not all at the same time, of course.

Even the smallest garden can include a number of vines because, of course, they need very little ground space. With any luck at all (and lots of compost) in a few years, the small gap in the fence I'm leaving open so the kids can come through to get their lost balls will be secretive and hidden.

Like a fairy gate. Sure and, wouldn't I love to have fairies living in the garden! Like the children, there's no point in trying to keep them out if they really want to get in, so you might as well make them welcome.

I wonder what plants attract fairies?

26.

On Becoming My Mother

YOU ALL KNOW THAT I PROMISE myself a rose garden. I've made a few starts—planted roses in two gardens and on an apartment balcony, and then left them behind as I moved on. I love my new home in my garden flat and even though I may not spend the rest of my life here, I will start again.

So when M.G. asked me what I would like for Mother's Day (I confess I didn't even question why he would be buying me a Mother's Day gift; I'm not foolish enough to look a gift horse in the mouth), I consciously ignored the fact that I may not have enough sun to keep roses happy and said immediately, "A rose bush," because that's what I always gave my mother and that means Mother's Day to me. Besides, with my mother gone and my daughters away, I reasoned, I deserved a treat.

Off we went to my favourite nursery to choose my very first David Austin rose. "Choose two," he said, and I ultimately chose three because I wanted to buy myself one in memory of the woman whose love of roses I inherited.

I was well prepared. Winter days and nights spent inhaling rose books enabled me to convince myself that, although not ideal, my conditions could keep some roses reasonably happy. Making lists ensured that I sort of knew what I wanted. I also sort of know what I don't want. I may change my mind sometime, but right now I don't want reds. Period. I want yellows and buffs, apricots and peaches, whites and creams, and colours of soft sunsets and blushing babies, but no reds. I don't want hybrid teas or floribundas. I want the roses Renoir painted and ramblers and climbers and maybe some ground-covers.

David Austin roses are sometimes called English roses, the result of the breeder hybridizing old-fashioned roses with modern ones. These have the appearance of old roses and the disease resistance of newer ones. Most are repeat-flowering and very fragrant. They sound like a good place to start before I get into true heritage roses, and are easier to find.

I chose Heritage, Graham Thomas, and Abraham Darby, in that order. Heritage is described in my books as "the perfect English rose" and "the one you would pick if you could only grow one." It has an upright habit and may reach 6 feet. The fragrant cup-shaped blooms are shell-pink shading to almost white and repeat well into the fall.

Graham Thomas is about the same height, but more arching in

form and may develop climbing-type canes or be trained as a pillar rose. The tea-scented blooms, which are deep yellow and peony-shaped, start early and finish late.

Abraham Darby is taller still, with large old rose-shaped blooms, coppery-apricot blending to yellow and pink. The growth habit is described in all my books as vigorous and robust, arching and spreading if not supported.

I chose these three, but I didn't bring them home yet. The nursery has lots of strong healthy specimens and they'll come along a lot faster in the greenhouse there until I'm ready to plant them.

I'll probably go visit them every week. How much we become our mothers! Her observations about the condition of Abraham Lincoln or Queen Elizabeth echo in my mind even as I write this. I used to get such a kick out of it; "Herbert Hoover didn't come through the winter very well."

My new friends aren't the hybrid teas and grandifloras that she loved, but I'll hear you, Mom, every time I comment on Abraham Darby or Graham Thomas. Considering how many roses are named after people, I'll slowly become my mother's daughter in yet another way.

"I do quite admire William Baffin, although he looks like a bit of a rogue."

Playing with Rocks

IT'S A FUNNY THING when you buy an old garden like mine. Even if there is little or nothing in it by way of ornamentals, it has a way of talking to you and telling you what it wants. The secret is in knowing how to listen, both to the garden and to your inner self. I flatter myself that I've learned to do the latter, although old conventional wisdoms and ideas do die hard. As for the former, you kind have to put aside what you heard in previous gardens when you move to a different one.

I did a lot of listening this week. With a little patio built, thanks to M.G., I got a better sense of traffic patterns and views. I rethought some of my plant wish list. I started laying out a path outline with old bricks I salvaged last year from a renovation down the street. I also made a mental apology to the spirit of my garden. In former columns I have denounced my soil and cursed the rocks. I am full of remorse.

The two sections in the front of the house are still hard and full of rocks and deserved to be cursed, but the soil away from the perimeters in the back is black loam, and joy, oh joy, full of worms. I was digging away out there, trying to think of anywhere else that I would be so happy to see worms and couldn't come up with a single place.

There are still lots of rocks, but even the rocks are wonderful: big round boulders that split easily, with a little encouragement from a pickaxe, into lovely flat paving stones. With the ones I already have, there are enough, I think, to do my paths, steps, and maybe even a small area adjoining the patio.

I'm happily scouring my books and stacks of old magazines for ideas. Not that I don't already have plenty, but as the bones of the garden take shape, I'm like a child at Christmas, wearing out the pages of the Wish Book.

Practically speaking, going through stacks of old magazines for articles I remember reading years ago (I just know there's one on brick paths set right down into the dirt) can be a bit frustrating, so I'm finally trying to be a little organized. Now as I'm going through old magazines, I'm cutting out articles that interest me, and punching them for ring binders. Next, I'm supposed to decide on categories and file them so I'll always be able to find what I want. This is the Martha in me. Knowing me, I'll probably never get around to filing them and will have odd pages tucked away everywhere instead of magazines.

Of course some of my magazines are almost old enough to be considered vintage, so I can't bring myself to cut them up, but I have to be tough with anything from the '80s and '90s.

Paths and steps absorb me this week. Most books tell you to install edgings and a layer of sand before putting down bricks or stones. I don't need that much work or even want the tailored look this would give my garden. My soil is well settled and so I think I'm safe to just set my material right in the ground.

First, I'll lay it all out. This will let me know if I have enough material before I start digging, and give me a chance to experiment with mixing the stone with the old brick. I like the idea of using these two textures and colours together.

Once I've got it all set up, I'll simply outline each piece with my edger, lift the soil, and set the stone or brick in place. I've walked on paths older than I am, done in this simple manner and still in place. They will suit the old cottage garden look and feel that I love.

The patio is ground level, and built of untreated spruce to save time and money. It's just 6 feet by 9 feet with a 4- by 6-foot bump. It cost $150 and M.G. put it up in one day. I will stain it charcoal to match the accent colour I plan to use on the house. Pressure-treated would last longer, but do I care? It's not supposed to be good for you and this deck will be good for at least twenty years and probably longer.

I can only hope I do as well.

28.

Old Friends/
New Friends

JUNE 2001

When you've practically started from scratch and you want an overgrown kind of garden, you need either lots of quite mature plant material or lots of patience. I can't afford the former and was not blessed with the latter, but even if I had pots of money and could go out and buy everything I want right now, my eventual garden wouldn't be nearly as dear to me as it's going to be because like most good gardens, it's going to contain lots of friends, some of them quite well travelled.

I brought some of Aunt Gladys's snow-in-summer from her garden in Gander with me to St. John's from my garden in Stephenville. Baby Sister and B-i-L donated common chives, old-fashioned bleeding heart, and Uncle George's geum, which came to their St. John's garden from his garden in Corner Brook. Baby Sis laments that she didn't get Mom's gardening gene or they'd have more to contribute. Their neighbours tell me they have lots of foxglove, some sedum, and other stuff. B-i-L's sister asked me over for garden advice and I came away with ivy, bachelor buttons, sedum, and a rollaway bed (not of the garden variety but for Daughter #1, who returns home on Friday from working in Ireland).

The first "new" contribution came from a Downhomer reader who sent me seeds for lavatera and pink poppies. A woman I'd just met cheerfully dug up pieces of day lilies, phlox, bleeding heart, rugosa rose, and feverfew on a freezing spring day. She also potted up stems of a tobacco willow, and this morning she announced she's got a bunch more stuff for me. I've never heard of tobacco willow and I have no idea if I want it or what I'll do with it. Sandy got it from someone who got it from someone who got it from Ireland. The white phlox she's given me is from England. That's the wonderful thing about shared gardens.

My next-door neighbour has given me enough day lilies to line both sides of the front walk. These have a history that I figure should make them feel right at home at my place. Marguerite, who also says she is not a gardener, rescued them when the hundred year old Victorian building across the street—the former poorhouse!—was demolished thirty-five years ago. That makes her a gardener in my books, not to mention the bedding plants and hanging baskets with which she beautifies her front yard every summer. She's been giving me something nice to look at for two years now and this year, hopefully, I'll start to pay her back.

Our spring has been so late that, as I write this at the beginning of June, there's still plenty of time to be moving perennials. I don't worry much about timing in moving perennials anyway. If you do move something at the wrong time, the worst that happens is you set it back a year. That's not a good enough reason to turn down a garden gift. If there's much foliage, it's a good idea to cut it back to give the roots a chance to establish and, of course, get the biggest root ball you can.

I wouldn't actually have bought some of the things I'm being given because they don't really fit into my gin-and-tonic garden plan, but what odds? I'll give everything a chance to prove it can thrive with some benign neglect and just pass on anything that sulks too much to a more vigilant gardener.

I'm not ready to plant all my treasures, so I've potted them in—guess what?—compost from the Whip-Pit! It actually made some over the winter and I'm still not sure how. I can see I'm going to have to get more pots. Sharing gardeners are everywhere; just walking to work this morning, I got offered more plants, solved a mystery, and learned a new tip.

A new neighbour a few doors down tackled a thickly overgrown old hedge and produced quite a pile of brush. I noticed that Louise, his neighbour and a gardener who has as little use for grass as I do because she dug up her whole front lawn last fall, took said brush and spread it all over her yard. I couldn't for the life of me figure out why. This morning she told me it's to keep the neighbourhood cats and dogs from turning her yet-unplanted garden into a giant litter box! It makes sense; no animal is going to dig or squat in a layer of prickly hedge trimmings.

29.

Good Bones Make Great Gardens

THANKS TO BRENDA from down around Chester, NS, way (who was once a Wells and is therefore considered kinfolk) for e-mailing me some tips about how to look after Abraham Darby, one of my new David Austin roses.

I am so grateful! I haven't planted him yet, and her tips may well make the difference in whether he and I have a good relationship. If he turned out to be sulky, as Brenda alerted me he could, I would have been quite disappointed in him. Now I know that I have to plant him with his graft well below the soil surface, protect him from the noon sun, and give him something to sprawl on.

Experimenting to see what will be happy in different parts of the garden is part of the fun. Every time I look out of my kitchen window, I see that forget-me-nots are very happy in my garden. I don't remember planting them, but there they are. I love their airy, bright blue in early summer and they are quite welcome to pop up wherever they like, which is obviously exactly what they do.

I bought another of my "must-haves," a flowering quince, and have to decide where it's going to settle in best. The quince is not particularly remarkable most of the year, but I love its spring display so much that I don't care. The one I found is large and well-branched, marked "orange," but is clearly going to be more like red. I wasn't going to have any red in this garden, but for the quince I make an exception. Its stiff, spiky twigs and branches are so beautiful for cutting and for forcing in early spring, and have a distinct oriental flair.

After days of experimenting, I've finished laying out the path from the little patio to the back of the garden, as well as stone steps up to the small level area at the bottom of the steep bank. I tried a number of different combinations of stone and brick and different curves to the path before I got something I liked. It's all laid out, but nothing is set permanently in place yet, and so I still have plants waiting patiently to be planted.

I finally decided to do the path completely with the old bricks I had and make the steps using the big flat stones and once I get the stones set in place, I'll experiment with some brick risers or tie in the brick in some other way. Then I had the brainwave to use the rest of the stone to build a low wall on the level at the top of the steps.

I love it! It doesn't retain anything, just sits on the very edge of the level area before it starts to slope and absolutely defines the whole upper area. Because of it and the curved brick path and stone steps, the garden has already taken on a wonderful new look.

I keep going to the kitchen window and looking out just for the pleasure of admiring the garden's new bones. Maybe it's the quince, but I can't help but think of minimalist Japanese gardens even though I'm definitely not a "less is more" type of gardener. I want everything lush and overgrown, but a well laid-out garden with good architectural features can stand on its own with nothing but one or two types of plants or just grass, or even sand in the oriental style. My stone wall is lovely all by itself, even though in my mind's eye I can already see ivy growing through it or maybe thyme tumbling out from the cracks.

If you're one of the many gardeners who spend lots of time and money at the nurseries and have lots of plants and flowers but never quite get the look they want, pay attention to the architectural features, or lack thereof, in your garden. That's what gives your garden style. I know I keep repeating that, but even this year in my own garden it has been driven home to me once more with the path, steps, and stone wall.

So if you can't quite put your finger on what's missing from your garden, think structure: paths, low walls, gates, benches, arbours, trellises. Picture your garden with no plants and you'll see if it has an interesting skeleton. If it doesn't, then that's where I'd put my attention for a while.

30.

No Elves for Me

I HAVE QUESTIONS TO ASK and a strong need for reassurance. First, the questions. I've been given a few odd-sounding perennials that I'm not familiar with, and can't find in my books. I know I might find them on the Internet, but I'd much rather ask real people, thank you very much. There's nothing as good as testimony from people in your own region who have tried the plant themselves, as I proved once more by last year's blue poppy question.

The mystery plants this week are sheeps' bit, Arctic hare, and milk-weed. These from the same woman who gave me tobacco willow, but she does have lovely ordinary stuff too, like black-eyed Susans, which I love so much I could almost fill the garden with them, except then I wouldn't have room for the other stuff I love so much.

Another one I am familiar with, but can't find, is goat's beard. If I ever knew its botanical name, I've forgotten it. It's a very useful land-scape plant for a gin-and-tonic gardener with shade. I used to admire it every summer by the side of a house down the street from me back in Former Life. In that location it died back to the ground every winter. I don't even remember at what time it started to bloom, but I do remember the masses of large, creamy white plumes on full-leaved plants about 3 to 4 feet high. I remember thinking it looked like a giant astilbe, and marvelling at how fast it grew back every year. I find it odd that I've never noticed it anywhere else, and I'm wondering if this plant has a dark secret that I should know about.

I can't think what it would be. It seemed very well-behaved in my neighbour's garden, and with small children and pets, I don't think they would have had something toxic around. Unless they didn't know....

That's it for the questions. Now comes the fun part, sort of, and why I'm in a bit of a dither and looking for reassurance. Next month I am going to be finally filming the pilot for a proposed *Gin-and-Tonic Gardener* television series on CBC.

God knows I've had long enough to think about it. I've known about it since the fall and it's been scheduled and cancelled a number of times because of weather already. Now they say we're going to do it in July no matter what the weather. (Good plan in St. John's, I'd say.) However, this week alone the starting day has been set, changed, then changed back again. And after I changed my hair appointment! Don't these people understand priorities?

I'd rather write about the garden than do television again, but it would be a good chance to pay the bills. The longer I have to think about it, the more I feel that I want it to be realistic, like the column. It always bugs me how most gardening or cooking or decorating shows make things look so easy. Nothing ever fails, and they start something, and before the show is over, you see the wonderful finished product. I find myself muttering, "Yeah, it's easy for you because when the cameras aren't on, the elves come in and do everything."

For the segments of the show that involve "doing," I don't want to have elves. This means that for some of the stuff, you won't see the beginning and the end on the same show, but isn't that reality? The good side is that if you want to see how something turns out, or even try it yourself at the same time and compare results, you'll have to keep tuning in because the show, in effect, will be like a serial.

The producer is not that sure, but I'd feel like a phony with elves. Anything that I can't do myself (and without too much exertion) has no place on a "Gin-and-Tonic" gardening show. I think gardeners are ready for more reality. What do you think?

Two Heads are Definitely Better

I HAD A REAL GARDENER VISIT ME the other day, and when I say real gardener, I mean a professional horticulturist and nurseryman, Newfoundland media gardening guru, Ross Traverse. Ross is going to be part of the TV pilot and he came for an informal brainstorming and rehearsal of sorts, so I got to parade my garden plans and dreams in front of him as we sat on my little back deck, sipping fake gin and tonics. (It *was* early in the morning after all.)

He encouraged me about some things and discouraged me about others and gave me all kinds of good tips and suggestions. What struck me the most was no matter how much you garden yourself and read about gardening and watch gardening shows and think you know a few things, there's nothing like an up-close-and-personal encounter with a real expert right in your own garden.

What it helps you to do is see your space through a different pair of eyes. Take the bank between me and the neighbour on the uphill side of me; it's about 25 feet long by 8 feet high and too steep to walk up. At the top is a line of young maple and birches on the neighbour's property.

Even though I pride myself on being able to think outside conventional wisdom in the house and garden, I couldn't seem to stop thinking rock garden for that bank. I admire good rock gardens, the natural looking kind with big rocks, but the idea hasn't really been turning me on for this garden, and I sort of had put dealing with the bank near the bottom of my mental list for that very reason. You know, I've even been thinking about faking a root cellar there just for fun and architectural interest and I guess just for something to do.

Ross liked that idea, but pointed out that with a small piece of culvert or something similar dug into the bank, I could just as easily have a real root cellar, since I planned to make the door and front frame anyway. He also advised me to cover the whole bank with a low shrub, and just one species, and right away I knew he was right. Sort of. He's right about using low shrubs instead of making a rock garden because it will require much less maintenance and will fit the natural, casual look I want. He's probably right about using only one species, but that's going to be a tough one for me. I will try keeping it down to two species, or three, definitely not four.

He also suggested planting high-bush cranberry somewhere because I want fall colour and to attract the birds. I may use that close to the top of the bank where it will provide a good privacy screen and I've written low-bush blueberry and honeysuckle on my list of other possibilities. I love cotoneaster *Horizontalis* for its enthusiasm, its fall colours, and bright red berries, but I should talk myself out of it for that bank because all the leaves from the neighbour's trees will get trapped in it and torment the life out of me. I am going to use it on my front bank, though.

Another thing that Ross pointed out is that I have nothing evergreen in the garden yet, and in our climate deciduous trees and shrubs are only in leaf for five months. So far I have nest spruce, holly, and Baltic ivy on that list. Growth can be contained by pruning, and pruning is my favourite garden thing (next to reading in something swaying, swinging, or rocking), so come fall maybe I'll find two nice native white spruce and plant a Christmas tree for the front and the back.

The last suggestions were about my maples: Take out six more of the lower branches on the big one in the back to increase my sun, and replace the smaller one in the front with a small flowering crab.

Sounds good to me, but I won't forget the most important thing about advice, even expert advice: You can pick out the parts you like and modify the rest because, after all, it is your garden.

32.

Somebody Stop Me

MOVE OVER GROUNDHOG DAY, it's Ground-cover Week. I have taken the first steps to banishing grass from my front garden forever. "Garden" is a bit elegant for two unfenced patches of grass dissected by a short concrete walk, but what would you call it? "Yard" seems too big. My computer thesaurus doesn't even give an alternate for "garden." The best Roget can do is "tract for flowers or horticulture." Anyway, it's a moot point because after this week, hopefully I'll be able to use the word "garden" without feeling like an imposter.

After a few hours of hard labour, about a quarter of the downhill side of the walkway, the side with the concrete retaining wall, is ready to plant, as is a section of the bank on the uphill side. So why haven't I gotten rid of all the grass with the easy lasagna method as I had planned, you might ask? Despite a little garden budget for the pilot, there is still that major drawback to that easy newspaper/topsoil layering method: the cost of the topsoil. The piles of newspapers are reaching alarming proportions, but despite my optimism, topsoil has sifted down to about number ten on my budget priority list and I'm having trouble getting past number five.

So, in my perpetual determination to find the silver lining, I have decided that this is not totally a bad thing because it gives me a chance to try different things and see what works best before I invest more time and money planting up the whole space, which I'd sort of have to do if it was a blank canvas of topsoil. This positive thinking stuff can be a bit of a stretch when your back muscles are stretched to weeping from digging, but the gin and tonic at the end of the day invariably helps.

I had decided on periwinkle (*Vinca minor*) as the main groundcover, but have had second thoughts because I'm told it can take much longer to establish in our climate than some of the others. I still want it because I love it, but I think I'm going to also have sweet woodruff (*Galium odoratum*). Both flower in late spring/early summer.

Periwinkle has dark, glossy trailing foliage with a blue, white, or purple flower, even though I've never seen the white anywhere. Sweet woodruff has lighter, upright foliage and a white flower. I think they'll work well in adjoining masses, and if I can't keep the woodruff from taking over, so be it. I'm hoping if I plant less of it and keep it well away from the periwinkle, they might just get along, and I'm even thinking of trying to design wavy growth areas with sunken edging (although I may lie down until the feeling goes away, in the hammock, of course).

I've also been given a piece of silver lamium to try, and a clump of variegated bishop's weed (goutweed—*Aegopodium podagria*). In my experience, bishop's weed is so invasive that I'm not going to even try to persuade it to get along with less aggressive neighbours. Instead, I think I'll put it in along the little strip between the edge of the driveway and the bottom of the concrete wall. If anything will survive there and keep the grass away, it's bishop's weed, obviously not called "weed" for nothing, and it will have nowhere to invade.

I've put my yellow poorhouse day lilies on either side of the walk, and a Coral Beauty (cotoneaster *Dammeri*) at a corner of the up-hill bank where there's no retaining wall.

That was enough for the front for now and for this week, period, but then I came across a terrific one-day sale last week—perennial bulbs and roots for $1. Now three Christmas ferns, two lady ferns, and a bleeding heart (*spectabalis*, the old-fashioned spring-blooming kind of Grampy's garden) are in front of the verandah. Of course they won't do much this year. They should have been started months ago and they are a bit sad looking, but the price was right, and gardens, like Rome, are not built in a day.

Compliments of the same sale, two more bleeding hearts, two pink peonies, two rosy oriental lilies, a white calla lily, four packs of montbretia, and a pack of freesia have joined the family in the back garden. I've put the calla lily in a pot with the freesia and also potted up half of the montbretia. The only place I've ever seen these winter over in Newfoundland was in my Aunt Bessie's Corner Brook garden and I'll never be the gardener she was, so I'll be taking the pot in for the winter.

I know, I know; I'm falling off the gin-and-tonic garden wagon and intervention is needed.

Of Flow-blue China and Roses

ON MY WALL HANGS A COPY of *Warning* by Jenny Joseph, given me by Baby Sister and lovingly matted in an old solid oak frame given me by a solid oak friend. In this poem the writer warns that when she grows old, she will spend her money on "brandy and summer gloves and satin sandals and say we've no money for butter." Of course the poem has nothing to do with summer gloves; it's all about feeding your spirit.

God knows I am not a frivolous spender by nature. Maybe I could be if I had the wherewithal to indulge myself, but I have a very practical side of which I am justly proud. I'm also kind of proud when people say Jenny Joseph's poem suits me.

Further along the same wall as the poem is my collection of flow-blue china, some of it chipped, none of it costly at the time, and all of it bought with money that could have been used for something more practical like winter boots. The treasure of that collection is a four-piece set of a shaving mug, soap dish, hair dish, and water jug; the basin is missing.

I happened to be in a South Shore antique shop just as it came in. I couldn't believe my eyes as the owner unwrapped the huge, perfect jug. She wanted $160 for the set. I knew the jug alone was worth more than that, but I had $20 to my name. Newly separated and living well under the poverty line, I had no choice but to get in my car and just drive away.

I suppose I might have made it about 10 miles before I turned the old car around, drove back, and asked the woman if she'd take a $20 deposit and hold it for me. I don't remember how I paid it off or how long it took me or what I had to do without. I do know that the set is worth many times what I paid for it, and I know that its value to me is priceless because every day of my life the beauty of it and the wonder that I actually own it feeds my spirit immeasurably.

I am telling you all this because I kind of did the same thing again this week. I bought shrub roses. Not as many as I wanted to because I didn't think the "$20 down to hold them" thing would work at the nursery, but still way more than I could afford.

It started when I got a call from a friend about a sale on roses at a nursery just outside of town. "Gorgeous," she said, "really healthy looking, full of buds, in 2-gallon pots for only $9.99 each." She bought three. She didn't know enough about roses to be able to tell me if they had the kind I wanted (and neither did the woman who answered the phone at the nursery!).

Of course I had to go investigate. She was right. They were gorgeous.

In fact they were the biggest, best-shaped, healthiest-looking roses I have ever seen. At first I saw only a few rugosas. Then I rounded a corner and there they were, spread out for hundreds of yards, all shrubs and climbers, perfect for M.G.'s place in a big meadow known as The Field.

M.G. has told me to pick out anything that I think would be nice at his place, but I've been a bit reluctant to take that step. He has terrific soil and full sun, so today I couldn't resist all the easygoing shrub roses I wish I could have.

I picked out sixteen and put them aside. Then I came home, and spent a lovely couple of hours looking them all up in all my rose books. I narrowed it down to ten. I was thus able to feel very sensible and virtuous while still thrilled with the indulgence of soul.

I don't know when I'll get out to The Field to plant them, so for now they're placed around the patio and along the old brick walk. I keep going out and looking at them: Heritage, Evelyn, Charles Austin, Jayne Austin, Rosa Mundi, Varigata de Bologna, Symphony, Kaleidoscope, Nearly Wild, and Climbing Handel.

There's another one I want, Golden Wings, but was afraid to buy because even though they were all big and vigorous, there wasn't a bud to be seen, while all the other varieties are covered. If someone can tell me that's not a problem and why, I'll be back out there in a flash.

34.

Not Exactly a Gin-and-Tonic Week

THIS HAS BEEN A HOT WEEK, the first full hot week of our summer. It was the kind of week that I would normally have been happily doing nothing in the garden except rocking, reading, sipping, and smelling the roses, which are opening beautifully. So, of course, this was the week they shot the pilot and the week Baby Sister decided she had to finally do something with her garden.

The pilot went smoothly enough and took only a day (you might know anything I'm involved with would be ultra-low budget) and Baby Sister's panic was partly my fault. I dragged her off to the nursery with me last week looking for roses to smell, and she ended up with as many as I did. The thing is, because mine aren't really mine but are destined for The Field, all I had to do was position the pots in my city garden.

She doesn't know what to do with hers. She's been asking me for ages to help her improve her back garden. I keep suggesting things, but she just keeps asking and not doing anything I suggest because what she really wants is for me to do it. She always jokes about Mom's gardening gene missing her and I've finally realized just how true that is.

There are some things that are so basic that even gin-and-tonic gardeners assume everyone knows them, like watering potted plants. Roses, potted or planted, don't need frequent watering, even in dry, hot conditions. What they need is deep watering because their roots are deep. Baby S. thinks she has watered these poor roses every day, but spraying them with the hose for 10 minutes just doesn't do the job.

I know it seems like you've been standing there a long time, but with the low hose pressure you must use so as not to wash the soil away, you'll find if you put your finger down in the container, it will be wet to maybe a couple of inches and that's all. It's better to take the nozzle off the hose, turn it down to a very gentle flow and place it in each pot, letting the soil get well soaked. You won't have to stand there holding the hose. You could read a chapter, switch to another pot, read a chapter, and so on. You'll also avoid getting the foliage wet which is always a good idea with roses, even those that are mildew resistant.

Anyway, a new home for her roses was needed without delay, so with a big piece of rope I laid a bed out on the sunniest side of her garden. It has fat curves and leads the eye naturally from the deck to the shed at the back of the garden. If the shed wasn't attractive, I'd have curved the bed differently, but it's a nice element in the garden, so why hide it?

Nephew #2 started taking off the sods and I sat down with a trowel to save every bit of topsoil. A quick chopping motion with the side of a trowel loosens the soil and breaks down the clods. I kind of like doing it; I find it relaxing and I love seeing the beautiful topsoil start to pile up.

She and I sat there, chopping, chatting occasionally, sisters sharing in the creation of a rose garden. We didn't get all the sods done, but I thought it was quite enjoyable and was looking forward to finishing the job the next day. Some chance—practically the minute I was out of there, she dumped the remaining sods into the compost, justifying herself over the phone to me by saying the topsoil wasn't wasted that way, which is true, of course, but what it said to me is that I will never make a real gardener out of her.

And so what? She'll never make a real housekeeper out of me. I feel a bit guilty that I obviously made her feel a bit guilty about that topsoil. She never makes me feel guilty about dust bunnies. We both love a type of beauty and order in the garden and in the house. That's the important thing, not how we achieve it.

Thanks to a reader for the information that Golden Wings likes to have a growth spurt and get well established before it buds. I went back and bought one.

Hear Me Purr

IT DOESN'T TAKE MUCH to make me happy. Saturday morning finding great garden stuff at the yard sales, hours of puttering in said garden, dinner with friends, and *Coronation Street* Sunday morning would have made my weekend contentedness cup runneth over, except that the issue of keeping grass looking reasonably respectable was raising its ugly head again.

I do have just a touch of envy for those urban rebels you read about who let their grass and weeds grow waist high in the face of neighbours' horror. They always talk about the principle of the thing and ecosystems and how they really like the natural look and I'm sure some of them mean it, but a little part of me always thinks they're just lazy and don't care how their place looks because if they did, they could have native grasses, trees, shrubs, and flowers that wouldn't just look like an abandoned mess.

The argument of beauty being in the eye of the beholder doesn't help me either because I don't think unkempt grass is beautiful. I've

Blanche Dubois-ed and Scarlett O'Hara-ed my way through the lawn-mowing issue shamelessly ever since I left F.U. depending on the kindness of strangers and sighing deeply and putting off thinking about it until tomorrow and provided enough students with enough pocket money to have bought myself a goat. For a while in Stephenville I did actually have the use of a grazing appaloosa mare, thanks to a truck-drivin', horse-lovin' beau, but it didn't last.

I haven't had much luck with my rotary push mower, which I thought was the ideal "mower for dummies." It doesn't run smoothly and is hard to push no matter how much oil I squeeze in around it. Something always goes wrong with the line or the feed when I whipper-snip and I've just accepted the fact that there's bad karma between me and machinery and grass. So after the yard sales on Saturday, when Baby Sister and I were out scouring second-hand stores for furniture for their new (eighty-year-old) summer place, and a truck unloaded a grimy electric lawn mower, I didn't even look at it in spite of my grumbling about grass to her not an hour earlier.

Baby S. pounced on it! For me! She's a little sick of my grass woes. We all are. We plugged the beast in. It purred like a kitten. We negotiated a price and a forty-eight-hour return deal, no questions asked, so I could try it out and bring it back if it was too tortuous. I figured I had nothing to lose and at least I'd have the grass mowed for another few weeks. So $40 later, I was the dubious owner of a Black & Decker, flip-handle, side-bagging lawn mower from the basement of a little old lady who hadn't used it for years.

I have to say, so far, that it was the best $40 ever spent on my garden. Brother-in-Law declared that the blade didn't have a nick and that despite the grime, the machine did look as if it had hardly been used. And it just started as easily as turning on a hair dryer. All I had to do was steer it.

I was like somebody with a new toy. I know this may sound pretty basic to most of you, but given my experience with temperamental gas cords and sputtering and stopping and starting, I am totally intimidated by lawn mowers. I know I can't be the only one who feels this way, so I have to share this triumph. Hear me roar!

I already had a long outdoor electrical cord even though I can't for the life of me remember why. I did the whole back yard, even the banks and knee-high stuff without a hitch, carefully keeping the cord out of danger. Then I did half of the front and decided to take a break for a well-earned glass of ice water.

That was a mistake. I lost my concentration. I was so tickled with myself when I jumped up to finish the job that I completely forgot about the cord and couldn't understand why my new best friend suddenly lost power until I saw the two severed ends in the grass. The man next door, probably watching because he was so amazed at the sight of me mowing, came right over and taped it together. I decided it was time for another cold drink, but I do confess that this one was just a tad stronger. Then I had a shower and got ready to go out for dinner.

The next day, I was feeling so good after *Coronation Street* and an hour of puttering that I decided to finish the job and didn't even get stressed when I ran over the cord again! Get this: I just dug out the electrical tape and a utility knife, sat in my old rocking chair, whittled away the insulator cover, matched up the colours, twisted and taped, got up, finished the mowing, and was so tickled with myself that I didn't even lose the mood when I turned the hose on the cordless phone and rendered it useless. I simply decided I didn't really need to talk to anybody anyway. Imagine thinking that anywhere else but in the garden!

36.

Nature's Garden in the Field

M.G. MOWS A LOT OF GRASS. In my mind's eye I've been picturing long, sweeping perennial beds here and, of course, roses. Wrong, wrong, wrong. Not the roses, but the traditional herbaceous borders are all wrong for here. The Field calls out for meadows and wildflowers. In fact The Field is already meadow and wildflowers, except for the part M.G. keeps mowed, and it's beautiful.

This morning I walked through it to pick a bouquet for the kitchen and counted eight kinds of flowers. The daisies, Queen Anne's lace, buttercups, and purple clover were easy to identify, but for the others I'm ashamed to admit I have to resort to my native flower book and that's back in St. John's.

I also found two great patches of low shrubby roses, about 12 inches off the ground, with no buds and no sign of having bloomed this year. They may be young offspring from the tall old double white that M.G.'s great-great-uncle brought from Nova Scotia to his grandmother at Sandy Point and now lives in his mother's garden just up the lane.

Sandy Point was a centuries-old hub of fishing activity in western Newfoundland and is now totally deserted. I'm fascinated to learn more about its history of French and English settlers from the Channel Islands, and am charmed beyond words to have been given carte blanche to dig up offshoots from this venerable old rose. I think it's probably a Blanc Double de Coubert, but again the reference books are back in St. John's.

And then maybe those low clusters discovered today, nestled among the tall grasses and flowers of The Field, are something different altogether—young rugosas, perhaps, from the masses down by the beach. The leaf is similar and the bird activity here in The Field is such that I expect I'll find even more of these dropped volunteers.

But back to the wildflowers (distracted by roses again); if I had a grain of sense I wouldn't even try to improve on the flowers here, and in essence I won't. I doubt I can convince M.G. to mow less and let the meadow come closer to the house, so I'll embrace the spirit of this wonderful natural garden, and not try to change it but maybe try to enhance it a little.

In the mid-'70s when, as a new bride and first-time homeowner, I started my first garden, wildflower gardens were in every magazine. I guess that was a natural progression from the flower-power days of the late '60s. There I was with an urban lot in a conservative neighbourhood, wanting nothing more than to fit in with all the other sensible young mothers whose evenings were filled with committees and sorority meetings and whose gardens all seemed to have globe cedars as the stars. I drew the line at sorority meetings, but I did get a cedar or two and certainly wouldn't have dreamed of setting the backyard to wildflowers, heaven forbid the front yard.

At the time, though, "they" made wildflower gardens seem so easy. There was a wildflower mix for every situation and all you had to do was scatter the seeds in the dirt, sit back with your macramé, and let nature take its course. I'm just as glad I didn't try it then because Mother Nature is no amateur, and turning one of her ecosystems into a wildflower garden that even remotely resembles the ones on the cover of the seed packages is not for amateurs.

Most of these packages have a mixture of perennials and annuals, with much more of the latter. The "meadow" might look good for the first year, but the annuals don't come back and even the perennials and the most determined self-seeders are hard-pressed to compete with neighbouring weeds and grasses. Emerging seedlings are easily overwhelmed by natives who've been the masters of their turf for years. In fact, giving the new plants two growing seasons in a nursery bed in order to get them ready for the territorial war isn't a bad idea.

You can see we're not talking instant gratification here. The collective wisdom that it takes at least three years to get a "natural" meadow established to the point where all you have to do is wander through in a Laura Ingalls hat, dreaming of a young Michael Landon.

In the meantime, while you're raising Olympic champion black-eyed Susans in an area protected from weeds, you're also supposed to be preparing the site by trying to kill all the existing vegetation. This is starting to sound like war, which I suppose it is, but there seems to be something intrinsically wrong with declaring war on an existing meadow so you can make a prettier one.

I'm wondering what if you just took the lawn mower and mowed a few curving swathes though the area, smothered the vegetation in the mowed sections and just planted the new settlers there. If they learned to co-exist happily, wouldn't you have the best possible meadow, with the natural flowers that you already enjoy enhanced with sweeps of other favourites?

Somewhere I have an article I saved because it was the best one I'd read on establishing a meadow. It took three years and, I think, involved a schedule of planting, seeding, and mowing, but was less daunting than the regime of cover crops, mowing, and tilling recommended by some books. One thing is for sure, the natural look can take a lot of work—just ask any woman.

37.

Be Still My Gardening Heart

AUGUST 2001

My garden cup seems to be running over. You might remember my laments that I've never had a man I could garden with. Not that one is necessary, mind you, but so many pleasures are better if you have someone to share it with and I've always wondered what it would be like to be able to have that feeling in the garden, not to mention the sharing of physical labour.

Former 'Usband dug the scattered hole, but our gardening time together was never what you'd even call congenial. Human disharmony in a garden is a profane thing, I think, and I don't think I could bear it again.

I've known M.G. for almost four years, but we haven't been what you'd call "in a relationship" for most of that time. When you're a re-single, slightly scarred baby boomer/third-ager, you shouldn't rush into these things. There are lots of things he and I don't have in common.

I've seen no evidence here in The Field that he's any kind of a gardener, unless you count all the neat mowing he does, which I don't really count, but it's better than having the place totally unkempt. He told me he used to help his father with the vegetable-growing, so I figured there was hope. He's so downright agreeable that I knew even if he took no real interest, he'd cheerfully help me with the heavy stuff.

Be still my heart! Yesterday might have been a very significant day. We started the rose garden. You might point out that the very fact that I decided to plant a rose garden in his field says something and you never know, but also who knows what second thoughts might have crept in if yesterday had turned out to be full of incompatibility and disappointment?

I carried all the pots out and started placing them around, just sizing things up. This took a while, during which time M.G. came back from cutting brush down by the river, eyed the roses scattered around the grass, and gave me a dubious look. I assured him I wasn't finished yet. That was the total extent of our garden disharmony.

I decided to situate the rose bed close to the house, all the better to enjoy the flowers up close. I have a rough plan for the whole property, which sounds more significant than it is—I just can't resist planning gardens. The back should be devoted to wildflowers, the front to shrub roses, and the sides to old-fashioned perennials—loosely, of course, because any garden I have anything to do with will always be a work in progress or, to borrow a wonderful phrase, a movable feast.

With the hose, I laid out a long, crescent-shaped bed across the front, with the inside edge of the thickest part about 12 feet out from where a verandah and sun porch might be some day, with a view to creating a sheltered enclosure there.

My back can't handle turning sod this week, and the soil here is too good to justify the lasagna method, so off I went to town for a visit with Janine, half hoping that M.G. might get at it, but not really expecting him to after a hot day working with the chainsaw.

Pleasant surprise no. 1: When I came back, he was almost finished taking up great slices of sod and knocking off the clods of reddish, somewhat sandy, and almost completely rock-free soil. Into the house I went to mix us a cold drink and do some supper things.

Pleasant surprise no. 2: When I came back he was DOUBLE-DIGGING, and wondering whether ten wheelbarrows full of the aged manure from the old barn up the hill would be enough.

And then, around dusk, I looked out and there he was, going at the still-potted roses with the hose. I certainly didn't tell him then that that's not the way to water roses. I was too busy counting my blessings and besides, there's lots of time to teach methodology. It's enthusiasm that can't be taught.

Not only that, it looks like he's going to teach me a thing or two. Apparently he used to grow big pumpkins "up behind Daddy's house," and informed me that throwing dishwater on them is the secret ingredient!

Who was it who said, "The way to a woman's heart is through her garden"? Oh, was that me?

38

Planting a Carpet of Roses

IT'S ONE THING TO KNOW what you want for a particular site, and sometimes it's quite another to be able to find it, especially in a rural area. I could say I was lucky last week. I could, but I prefer to think there was more to it than luck when I found just what I wanted to cover the sunny, exposed spot where my mother and father were laid to rest.

I'm fortunate not to have had much close experience with cemeteries. I know some that are more austere than others. Many have very strict regulations about not planting anything but grass, and about what types of markers are allowed. I'm so glad the place where we laid my mother's tired body isn't like that. I've never met anyone who loved flowers more than she did; just as much perhaps, but more would be impossible. And roses were her favourite.

It took me awhile to decide what I wanted to put there. It had to be low maintenance because neither my sisters nor I live close by. I am back and forth a bit visiting M.G., so they tactfully let me decide.

Grass was an obvious choice—the caretaker would keep it mowed—but I just couldn't bring myself do that, not to the woman whose garden made me think Jiminy Cricket was a character named after a rose instead of the other way around.

The hybrid tea rose I planted before Dad died survived only one winter. After his ashes joined her, I had a local nurseryman surround the site with a low wooden frame, stain it, and fill it in with topsoil. I got back there in the winter, but that was no good, so this recent trip was the first chance I've had to plant anything. I flew on the spur of the moment and there was no chance to check the St. John's nurseries and pack up something.

By this time I knew what I wanted—ground-cover roses. Funny how things seem so obvious once you make up your mind, but what were the chances I'd find them in early August in and around the small town of Stephenville?

None of the nurseries had any, neither did Wal-Mart or Dominion, and then there they were at Canadian Tire! Four—and only four—beautiful, healthy specimens of Flower Carpet roses, two pink and two white, full of buds and complete with packets of six-month time-release fertilizer.

Accompanied by my best friend Janine, and armed with four bags of manure compost from the old barn in The Field, plastic bottles of water, and two bags of shredded pine bark mulch, I finally finished this labour of love.

It's a beautiful site in full sun, overlooking rolling hills and a glimpse of the ocean. Mom would love the idea of a mound of roses, and Dad would be happy that she was happy.

I had to go to the library in Stephenville and refresh my memory on Flower Carpet. Holy cow! ... "extraordinarily attractive shining foliage"; "almost evergreen, lasting far into winter and sometimes spring"; "continuous flowering well into fall"; "disease, pest, wind, rain and salt resistant"; "tolerates part shade"; "easier to maintain than grass." They have semi-double blooms, lightly fragrant and profuse, and grow up to 30 inches high, spreading vigorously to almost 4 feet.

Not only that, they can be rooted by stem-pinning and sometimes do it all by themselves. My *Rose Atlas* lists seventeen references to Flower Carpet and calls it "one of the most successful garden roses all over the world in recent years." And there they were, just waiting for me in a small-town Canadian Tire, in my one planting window of opportunity, on a sunny day, with my old friend in tow.

Serendipitous all around.

39.

Gardening Ifs and Maybes, Irresistible

YOU'D THINK REDOING an old garden would be easier than starting from scratch on a wild patch. I would have thought so before I came face to face with M.G.'s acre of lawn in The Field. Now I see that somehow even a woodlot would feel much more of an inviting canvas than all this grass. There is lots of brush and small trees between the lawns and the river, and I've come to the startling realization that I'd just as soon tackle that as the cleared portion.

Intrinsic in our very souls is the idea that a garden is a spiritual place of peace and beauty—Eden, Paradise, Valhalla, to name a few—and I think people have an inner voice that tells them how their particular garden should be. Some people never hear the voice and for some of us the voice is stronger and I guess we are the ones who get out there and try to do something about our little corner of earth.

There's nothing wrong with the growth along the river, but if I lived here, I wouldn't be able to resist the urge to enhance it so I'd get more pleasure out of it. First I'd have to fight my way through it all and tag the things that I want to stay. Then all the dead and dying, overgrown, and overcrowding stuff would have to be removed.

I think the fact that that is less daunting to me than the cleared portion really defines my garden design instincts and style. The junipers, white spruce, and birch that would remain down there after the clearing would be the natural bones of that section of the garden. The ferns and grasses would be the muscles. I wouldn't have to make those decisions; nature has made them for me. I'd do a little muscle building, of course, but my main job would just be adding a little blush here, a little gloss there.

In the tamed cleared section, even the bones are gone. If there was even one nice tree, there'd be a starting point, an original bone, a living granddaddy for all the other strangers introduced to the garden to relate to.

The rose bed was a symbolic start, something I couldn't resist doing and I'd do it again, but it reminds me in a sense of how inadequate I am as a gardener compared to Mother Nature. It's a lovely bed and a nice improvement to blank lawn, but to me it looks very lonely. Even adding a finch feeder hanging from a natural curved spruce stake, and a bird bath, made from a large flower pot saucer filled with beach pebbles and water, to one end of the rose bed didn't help.

It's a difficult dilemma faced by gardeners everywhere. The hardscaping should be done first—decks, structures, paths—then the trees, shrubs, and perennials and annuals. (Did you notice that the expensive stuff comes first?) If you're planning a sun porch and a verandah, you don't want to start the paths until those things are done. You just don't know about natural traffic patterns until the hard elements are in place.

I know where I think some would be if I stayed here. Others would be determined by where I'd eventually put the arbour and the old-fashioned double swing and the hammock and the rain barrel and all the other stuff of garden dreams. I'd plant a flowering cherry, an apple, and a lilac, and I'd be finished with making lonely beds.

I can have a bit of fun with the meadow out back regardless of future plans or lack thereof, so M.G. built me a nursery bed. It's not large, but it will hold a lot of stuff for a short time. It backs onto the garage and is simply made from two pieces of 6-inch pine clapboard nailed to a series of 2-by-4 stakes in the ground. Of course the clapboard is too thin to last any time, but it was what he had on hand and enabled me to start some perennial seeds. It can be reinforced easily enough if it becomes a permanent fixture. I think I'd like the natural look of slabs. M.G. is a bit more conservative.

We used a sort of modified lasagna method for the nursery bed, layering the existing grass with wetted newspaper, then adding two layers of sods taken off the rose bed, upside down, before topping it off with a few inches of topsoil. I also spread a big bucket of compost scraps between the sods just for good measure.

The topsoil will be adequate now for seeds, and maybe next year the soil will be deep enough to use this bed for holding small shrubs and larger perennials. Who knows what the spring will bring?

To get the drifts of meadow flowers this property needs will require a lot of each species. I've started with three or four packs each of black-eyed Susans, purple coneflowers, scarlet and blue flax, and mistflower.

This last (*eupatorium*) is a new one to me. It's described as a "bold, easy-to-grow perennial with sweetly scented light purple flowers that provide a lure to butterflies." It's about 3 feet tall and recommended for borders or meadows.

Now that the holding bed is done, I'll be seeing what else I can find on my trip into Corner Brook today. The search and the fun never stop, even if it's not for your own garden.

Magazine Cover Material

SUDDENLY I'M IN NOVA SCOTIA on a flying visit. Even though I intended to be back in St. John's by now, I couldn't pass up a free ride and the opportunity to see Daughter #2, rationalizing that I'm already halfway there anyway when I'm on the west coast of Newfoundland, but it sure is frustrating not being in my own vehicle. For a person like me to be turned loose in the flea markets, garden centres, and yard sales of another province with no way to bring "stuff" back is a form of subtle torture.

I have pulled off some major coups in my time, like a huge wicker rocking chair and a stand-up steamer trunk and a longhorn steer skull complete with long horns (don't ask) while travelling by plane, but even I recognize the limitations of bus and ferry travel.

When my ride returned to Newfoundland, I just wasn't ready to leave Daughter #2 or Nova Scotia either, for that matter. With a last-minute, one-way airfare back to St. John's being in excess of $600, it was the bus and the ferry for me.

But even if Daughter #2 didn't have somewhere I could store it, I couldn't have passed up what was for me the find of the year. Of course the year isn't over yet, but I doubt I'll top this because it combines my love of the garden with my love of interesting and beautiful old things, *and* is useful *and* was affordable.

There I was, driving through Mahone Bay in Future Son-in-Law's car, on my way to visit my friend and writing guru in First South. You probably didn't know there was a guru in First South, but there is and his name is John and I'm just waiting for him to become rich and famous so I can get a job writing his RSVPs or dinner party menus or something.

Anyway, with Daughter #2 about to move into her first very own apartment, I was not in a mode for spending on myself, so I'd actually passed right by all the South Shore antique shops—no mean feat. But when I spotted a used-furniture store, I would have stopped even if I wasn't thinking about apartment furniture because long ago I discovered something interesting about such second-hand stores. They often have the same treasures that you might find in an "antique" shop at a fraction of the cost.

If you've read any gardening/decorating magazines in the past while, you have to know that garden antiques are all the rage. Every Martha Stewart wannabe and even the Definitely Nots have looked at a picture of a charming scene under an apple tree—little French bistro table set with old linens, mixed but matching china, and a vintage crock of vintage roses—and thought, "Where would I find stuff like that around here?"

Well, you could have found the bistro set in a Mahone Bay second-hand store last Thursday morning if you'd gotten there just before I did; a little iron and wicker table and two curlicued chairs, very heavy and in good shape, for $50!

I didn't have $50 on me and had left my bank card somewhere, so I actually drove away, telling myself that it would be too much trouble to get it back to Newfoundland anyway. Shades of flow-blue china, I got about a hundred yards and thought "Are you crazy?" made a U-turn, and went back.

There was a young couple sitting on *my* set deciding to buy it! What did I do, brazen hussy that I am, but march right past them and ask the owner if he'd take a deposit to hold it until the next day, which he did before they had a chance to open their mouths. It actually folded right up and fit in the trunk! In November Daughter #2 will bring it home. Next summer I'll have the roses and be able to set a table right out of *Victoria* magazine.

I missed out on some great shrub bargains, though, at the Sunday flea market in Lower Sackville. I knew it would make me unhappy to look too closely at stuff I couldn't have, and the Japanese maples and tall bushy hydrangeas for $10 are still on my mind. This is a good time for bargains anyway, but these seemed particularly good. I'm going to start checking out the stock around here today.

I did manage to bring back more than seventy ivy clippings from a visit to my uncle and aunt in Kentville. Uncle Don (whom I gather usually has the job of pruning) got a big kick out of me spending a part of my short visit with them trimming the ivy from around their big front window. To me it was an extra bonus, particularly as their ivy has a wavier leaf than the Baltic variety I planted this spring. They warned me not to grow it on the house like they did because it is rampant.

Mine is for my expanse of concrete retaining walls, so its vigorous suckering habit will be perfect. I soaked them overnight in a pail of water, wrapped them in wet paper towels, aluminum foil, and a plastic bag, and they made the long trek home just fine.

Mahone Bay also yielded what may turn out to be the best pair of gardening gloves I've ever had. They're called Watson Botanically Correct, are extremely comfortable, and seem tough, for under $10.

All together, with seeds gathered from friends and family (and a few single hollyhock pods I confess I helped myself to outside a house on Agricola Street), it was a pretty good garden trip.

41.

Hooked Again?

SEPTEMBER 2001

If you've ever thought that some of my musings are for the birds, I couldn't argue with you this week. I've got birds on the brain because they're so busy getting ready to travel. I've always liked watching birds, which is not quite the same thing as birdwatching. Birdwatchers are much more serious and informed than people who just enjoy watching birds when they happen to be around, or even people who make an effort to attract birds to their gardens.

Birdwatchers will tramp around in all kinds of strange places just for the mere possibility of adding another species to their life list. (I've never had this explained to me, but I imagine it's birdwatcher talk for species they have seen alive in the wild.) Somehow I can't see myself sitting still or skulking about in the cold or swatting flies for hours to get a look at a bird no matter how rare or beautiful it may be. But maybe birdwatching is a progressive addiction. If so, I could be in trouble.

I have three different kinds of feeders in St. John's: one I call a "regular" feeder hanging from a branch; one suctioned to a window; and a table feeder. There are lots of trees around for shelter, and I see and hear lots of birds, but they very seldom come to my feeders until the fall. I sit there on my deck, watching them through binoculars.

"It can't be me they don't like," I think. "It must be because of Connor the cat," even though the feeders are safely out of his reach.

Pete the cat lives in The Field. I hung one feeder out there just a few feet away from the living room window. It took a few days, but then a blue jay arrived. Soon, there were three regulars. Then the black-capped chickadees came calling.

One morning, in a ten-minute period, there were six blue jays, eleven robins, a pair of purple finches, two yellow warblers, four chickadees, two hermit thrushes, and what I think was a baby starling. I think it because I looked it up in my Audubon Society Field Guide after I examined it closely through my new Bausch & Lomb compact binoculars. See what I mean about progressive?

I bought the field guide years ago. This spring, I decided I couldn't stand another year without a good pair of binoculars. You know how it goes when you don't want something cheap and can't afford something expensive. Luckily for me, I have a friend in the bird business who offered me cost price and a quasi-dollar down and a dollar a week payment plan. How could I turn down such an opportunity?

Now, I'm going to have to get a new purse or knapsack of some kind because I want to take my binoculars everywhere I go, but I don't want them hanging around my neck all the time. I could clip them onto a belt, but then I would have to buy belts and stuff with belt loops and be constantly reminded that I don't have a waist.

And with a memory so bad that I sometimes manage to forget that, I figure what's the point of having my binoculars if I don't have my book on hand to look up the little feathered things when I spy them. Even when they're in my own garden, I have to check two or three times before I notice details like "white ring around the eye" or "white under tail coverts." Then I want to look up what a covert is, but I draw the line at carrying a dictionary around.

On the other hand, I'm overdue for a new bag anyway. The newest one I have was a gift from the horse beau who's had time to get married and have two children since the days he was professing undying love for me. I need one with different compartments that are easy to open and that will also leave my hands free.

Now that I think of it, I do have that lovely suede knapsack-style bag from South America that I can't bear to part with even though all five zippers are gone and the cost of replacing them is more than double what I paid for the bag ten years ago (and it was new, not yard sale). It's kind of heavy, though, and not for warm weather.

But back to the progressive addiction of watching birds. In The Field they come to feed early in the morning. There I am, lying in bed around 6 or 7 o'clock, ready for that warm schmoozy feeling that comes when you realize you can turn over and have another snooze, when I hear the birds and I have to get up because I'm afraid I'm going to miss something!

My St. John's friend in the bird business has bird plants and feeders situated right outside her big bedroom window so she can watch the show as soon as she opens her eyes. Now I have to rethink some of my garden ideas again. Either that or get rid of the binocs and the book and kick the habit before it gets too bad. Go cold turkey, as it were.

There's another bird reference. It may be too late.

You Never Know What You'll Find

THE THINGS YOU FIND WHEN YOU'RE WEEDING! One thing I didn't expect to find were potatoes in the front of the house where spuds have never been planted, but there I was, hauling out handfuls of weeds and unearthed some lovely little potatoes, still too tiny to eat, but they can stay there for another month or more yet.

There's a simple explanation, I guess. The compost I dug in there must have had small portions of potato peelings not quite decomposed, even though it wasn't obvious to the eye. Anyway, I'll get enough for one meal for myself, so that's sort of a fun bonus.

When the weather is nice in September, September is my favourite garden month. Everything is mature and lush. The weather can be sublime, warm and soft on your body without searing heat, a scent and promise of wood fire more imagined than real but comforting just the same.

Today Janine and I walked in the Botanical Gardens at Memorial University. A class of senior (in age, not necessarily proficiency) art students were there, easels and sketch pads, pastels and pencils, sitting on warm stone and smooth wood, each intent on capturing a petal or a pumpkin or whatever caught their fancy. It made me wish I had brought my modest art supplies so I could capture them capturing the essence of a dreamy late September afternoon.

The ivy I brought home from Nova Scotia and stuck in the ground seems to be doing just fine. This week I pegged down a couple of pieces of honeysuckle so that by spring I may have two new plants to transplant. I just bruised a node portion of a long stem and buried it under the soil, while leaving the stem attached to the main plant and about 8 inches of the tip exposed. I weighted down the buried portion with a rock, and that's all there was to it. This method works for any number of shrubs, and you've got absolutely nothing to lose by trying it.

Parts of my garden are looking pretty woebegone. Some of that is because it's been left to fend on its own for almost six weeks, but part of it is simply because it is getting to be that time of the year when some cleaning up is called for anyway. How much you do depends on how neat you are, I suppose, but this is one time where it really doesn't pay to be too obsessed with neatness.

Cutting off spent blossoms to keep the plant from producing seed during the season helps keep flowers blooming, but once September comes, I do the bare minimum. Many of those seed pods you'd be throwing away will become new plants next year if you leave them alone. They'll also provide food for birds and create winter interest as they catch the snow and make ethereal shapes.

If you want to pick some seeds to save, the standard advice is pretty simple. Pick them when they're ripe and almost dry, usually black or brown in colour, and place them in individual paper bags. When they're totally dry, you can store them in an airtight container and keep them somewhere cool and dark. When I get around to actually harvesting seeds, I put them in envelopes, label them, and then seal them in a freezer bag. Occasionally I even find them in the freezer the next year and get all excited.

Right now I'm all excited about my latest architectural find. There I am driving along a country road in Kilbride on my way to a yard sale, and I spy a large, semi-circular contraption of ornate iron on top of what seemed to be a pile of garbage on the side of the road. Of course I had to stop. It turned out to be the headboard for a round bed, circa

1960s. It was being thrown out and the owner graciously agreed to keep it to one side for a day or so while I figured out how to get it home.

So far I see it with a rose planted to one side and twining through it. That's as far as my mind's eye has taken me yet, but the possibilities are endless.

That's one of the joys of creating a garden.

Still Dreaming

DESPITE THE CONTINUING HEAT, I'm thinking of the fall and winter garden and I don't have enough out there to look forward to. For reds, I have Virginia creeper, burning bush, and cotoneaster, but they're relatively small. I'm not fond of the Autumn Joy (*Sedum spectabalis*) that is so popular around here or the flowering cabbage and kale that brightens many a fall and even winter garden, but I wish I had something more.

Dragging the mower over the back bank a few days ago convinced me that the sooner that particular patch of grass is gone, the better. Keeping Ross's suggestions in mind, I do want a casual, cohesive look for that bank and my criteria are low maintenance, fall colour, attraction for birds, and, of course, pleasing to my eye and spirit. Now that I've gotten rid of the rock garden imprint, my mind can't seem to shake the low cotoneasters. Their arching branches and fall colour and berries would be beautiful, but they aren't low maintenance in a garden that fills up with leaves every fall.

Virginia creeper would be nice and I have that one that has been sulking on the back fence for three years now. I might try a few blueberries too. They turn a lovely scarlet in the fall, and being able to pick blueberries might be particularly soothing if I'm city-bound in late summer.

Another plant group that has good winter interest is ornamental grass. There are so many of them so I was planning to do some homework, one of my favourite pastimes in front of the winter fire anyway. However, I'm remembering a tip I read somewhere about growing grasses in pots until you get a nice big clump and then planting them in the garden. I can't remember exactly why, but maybe I'll look around for some this weekend and pot them indoors. Of course you can still plant stuff right out in the garden, but I think a few extra weeks indoors will give them a head start on next spring.

I already have a yellow and a white ribbon grass. *Miscanthus* is probably one of the most common genus with numerous varieties available. *M. sinensis,* or silver grass, is said to be one of the more invasive ones. *M. sinensis purpurascens,* or red maiden grass, sounds good to me because it remains fairly compact and turns auburn in the fall. There's moor grass and oat grass and switch grass and feather grass and fountain grass and Indian grass and fescues and sedges and heaven knows what else.

If you already have ornamental grasses, it seems the best thing to do in the fall is just leave them alone. You may have to pull out some brown stalks in the spring just to tidy up the clump or patch, but for the most part they'll provide beauty of shape and colour through the winter. A lot of the grasses from the "carex" family, while technically not grasses at all, look like grasses and are evergreen or semi-evergreen. There seems to be more every year. How does one keep up?

My Wild Poppy

SOMETIMES I'M NOT SURE why I have such a compulsion to garden. I know somehow I have my mother to thank (blame it on?), but I also know I'll never be nearly as good at it as she was. She'd never have gone away and left her garden for six weeks the very same summer she dug up new ground and planted lots of new stuff, but not lots enough to crowd out the weeds. At the very least she would have mulched everything first.

I, on the other hand, thought little of swanning off, leaving great fertile gaps of soil between plants. I might as well have put up a sign saying "Bed and Breakfast for Weeds." Of course there were any number of reasons why, after spending so much time digging and enriching my soil, settling in all my new plants, I then abandoned them to fend for themselves. I (a) left in a hurry; (b) didn't have any ready mulch and didn't have the means or the muscle to get the bought stuff; (c) I just didn't get around to it; (d) I had other time and spending priorities; (d) all of the above, which is the right answer.

It's all perfectly all right; I make no bones about my gin-and-tonic approach to gardening; anything that can't stand being left to fend for itself every now and then doesn't belong in my garden anyway. It's another reason to try only one or two of anything before spending much money or effort on it; determining the survival of the fittest.

But every now and then, like when I come home to a bumper crop of chickweed and all the company it keeps, I can't help but imagine my mother's disapproval. Then I sort of become a guilt-ridden little girl again and that's when the "Why do I do this?" thoughts creep in.

Not "Why do I neglect the garden sometimes?" That's only mild guilt and I've already explained why I do that. No, I get right down to "Why do I even have a garden at all if I'm not going to look after it better?" Then I have a day like yesterday and I know why I want a garden and I am so thankful for it and I know even if I did my very best with the garden, it would still do some things independent of me and what I want it to do.

Daughter # 1, my first baby, my roaming child who has lived in foreign lands but has been home with me this summer, is leaving this week to spend a few months with her boyfriend who is already there, in a land that suddenly seems more foreign than any of the others: the United States. New York City, to be exact.

This was planned long before the horror of what happened on the eleventh day of this ninth month and I wasn't real happy about it then. I hoped and prayed, of course, after the terror of September 11 that she'd change her mind, but by yesterday morning I knew she wasn't going to and a black cloud settled over my heart.

I had some pressing business to take care of and I couldn't remember the details. I tried to write; I couldn't even think. I tried to shop; I just stared at the shelves. I tried to work around the house; I just wanted to get into bed and pull the covers over my head.

It was a beautiful day. I poured a cup of coffee and sat in my rocking chair, staring at the garden. The coffee got cold before I finished it. Then I went almost mindlessly inside, opened the bottom drawer and pulled out a T-shirt and a clean pair of gardening overalls. I weeded and clipped and pruned and transplanted until my hands and nails and overalls were ground in with dirt, and then I was calm.

Calm and accepting the fact that some flowers just won't, or can't, grow where you want them to and a smart gardener shouldn't try to harness them. A smart gardener will admire their strength and beauty and do whatever she can to help them thrive, but know when to let them go. If I didn't have a garden, maybe I wouldn't have remembered yesterday how much I love wild poppies and how I really wouldn't try to change them, even if I could.

Garden Lessons

OCTOBER 2001

This week my garden reminded me of yet another reason why I love gardens. To say it's been a troublesome week for me would be a bit of an understatement. Ditto last week, although I kept it at bay. Despite my introspection about wild poppies and good intentions, I kept lapsing into despair about my daughter going to New York.

I was so low that I even lost interest in the garden. Everything I had out there was pretty well finished anyway. If you remember, almost half of everything I planted this year in the St. John's garden was given to me by friends, so I had little input there into making sure I had fall colour and I didn't seem to be thinking of it when I was buying whatever was a bargain.

But I also didn't really know everything I had, and the day after my wild poppy left, I discovered two clumps out there covered in tiny rosy buds and now I have two lovely bunches of deep pink—

fuchsia really—New England asters (or Michaelmas daisies), admonishing me for giving up too soon, telling me that it's not over 'til it's over.

Not only that, but farther down the brick path, all around one of the old tree stumps, the annual malva zebrina that I cut down a month ago because it was so tall and scraggly is bushy with new leaves and loaded with new blossoms, smaller than the originals, but just as bright.

Monday was still mercifully, beautifully warm. I took my coffee out to my rocking chair by the kitchen door this morning and the sun warmed my listless body while the garden, once again, warmed my spirit.

I plucked one, just one, of the aster flowers, and was surprised at the dismay I felt when I discovered two more buds right underneath. I couldn't bear to lose one little blossom, and floated the three of them in a flat little glass candleholder, where the buds seemed to be winking at me.

How could I have forgotten how much I love New England asters? I had to run to my books to look them up and read about them again. The most interesting reference is in my *English Cottage Gardens* book by Edward Hyams. Michaelmas daisies is the English name, and they're described as a "thoroughly cottagey flower which began to reach England as early as 1633," which, of course, makes me think they probably originated on this side of the ocean because we have so many wild varieties.

"Most of the cultivars we are familiar with were the products of 19th-century nursery work, and the dwarf forms didn't reach their present perfection until the 1930s." They're a perfect choice for my St. John's garden, where I want spring and fall bloomers because I hope never to have to spend another summer in the city.

Marjorie Harris, in *Favourite Garden Tips*, says her fall garden "glows with just about ... any Michaelmas daisy I can get my hands on." They flower late, on full, bushy plants, and are very fast-growing.

James Crockett, in *Crockett's Flower Garden*, recommends giving them lots of room (which, of course, means they'd be better suited to the big garden in The Field), but I must accommodate a few more varieties here as I may never be out there in the fall. Crockett says they'll double in size over a year. Some varieties, like the well-known Harrington's pink, can grow up to 4 feet, but early pinching will control this somewhat, and produce more flowers. He says the seeds aren't sold because they never breed true, which may not still be true because my book is a 1981 publication, and I'm sure I've seen seeds for sale.

At any rate, I have to get more of them because while I was reading Crockett, with my mind mercifully distracted from Ashley for a few minutes, the phone rang and it was herself, distraught because after waiting three days in Montreal, she was refused permission to enter the United States. It seems "joining my boyfriend to tour the States for a couple of months" didn't impress border officials in these traumatic post-9/11 days.

I tried to sympathize, but of course I didn't really, and New England Asters will forever be related in my mind with good news and "it's not ever over 'til it's over."

Tried and True Gin & Tonic Friends

Shrubs

John Cabot rose
One of the Explorer series that seems indestructible. Janine has had one in a partially shady corner almost overgrown by grasses and weeds and it keeps blooming every year. With a minimum of attention I'm sure it would reach its possible height of nine feet.

Potentilla Abbottsford
I always found potentilla a bit insipid until I succumbed to this white one covered in glorious bloom and planted it in a big pot. I go away and leave it for weeks without water; it can look dead but I'll clip it and tuck the pot somewhere less noticeable and it keeps bouncing back and forgiving me.

Japanese Quince
As long as it has enough sun it will take your breath away every spring and remind you why you garden.

Cranberry Cotoneaster
A groundcover or specimen for banks, it survives road salt. Not wholly g & t because its almost evergreen arching sprays can trap autumn leaves and look really messy but I love its sturdy gracefulness, fall colour and bright red berries so much that I don't mind cleaning it up a bit.

Clumping perennials

Daylilies
Will never sulk no matter what you do. The old orange ones can look a bit gawky with their giraffe-like stems but I love them anyway, especially at a distance. They even make good low hedges or borders. The newer ones, and there are hundreds if not thousands, are more compact. You could grow nothing but daylilies and have a beautiful garden all season, except you won't have cutting flowers; the blooms don't last.

Bleeding heart
The newer fern leaf one, eximia, is smaller and blooms much longer, but the older one, spectabalis is the sentimental favorite from your grand-mother's garden. Can get quite large and look spectacular all by itself in the late spring/early summer.

Peonies
Once they're planted happily, peonies can live for a hundred years with you or without you. Mine have done well in sun or part shade and mediocre soil with no fussing. They're messy but worth it I think.

Veronica	You can ignore it completely in almost any soil in sun or part sun and be rewarded with clumps of white, blue or pink spires that add reliable color for months and are great for cutting. I'm grateful enough to ignore the cat pee smell when you touch the leaves.

Spreading perennials

Snow-in-summer	I love it tumbling over a rock wall. The masses of small white flowers are perky and have a lovely scent and the grayish green foliage looks good all season, especially if you dead-head after it blooms in early summer. Not for lawn people; it can get out of control.
Ajuga	Will carpet a bank or shady difficult area and is easier to control. The common green-leafed one puts on a striking blue flower display for a couple of weeks in the spring. I don't find the variegated one as hardy, nor it and the chocolate varieties as pretty.

Re-seeders

Forget-me-nots	Another early bloomer. Some years are better than others because it is a biennial. Mine starts to gets mildewed after it goes to seed so I just pull it up secure in the knowledge that it will pop up somewhere else again next year.
Feverfew	An over-enthusiastic self-seeder but worth it because it will keep on going in spite of you. You just have to keep pulling up the volunteers you don't want. It seems cruel and wasteful at first in a garden that encourages independence but you will learn to be ruthless.
Foxglove:	Another one that pops up wherever it pleases. I love this old cottage garden flower and am so appreciative of independent plants that I just transplant the ones that are in really inconvenient places, like the middle of a path.

There are many more, but we each have to find the ones that work for us, so we don't have to work so much ourselves.